KW-442-103

Acknowledgments

Special thanks to John Thompson, R.G.N.(Hons.) who patiently read each section as it was written and who advised me on all the anatomical and physiological details. Grateful thanks to Leana Pooley who edited the finished manuscript and curtailed my commas. Special gratitude also to my Publishers Aardvark Press and Albert and Sarah Thiel who have taken such a personal interest in this work and who have never failed in their encouragement.

Dedicated

to all my students, past and present

and to Evelyn Laye

With my love and sincere gratitude for her unceasing encouragement and belief in my work.

JOHN DALBY

How To Speak Well In Business

Illustrated
by
the Author

How To Speak Well in Business
John Dalby

© Aardvark Press and John Dalby, 1993

First Printing
August 1993

10 9 8 7 6 5 4 3 2 1

Edited by: Leana Pooley
Music Printing by Carver's Perfect Score, Las Cruces, NM
Original tape recording made by Nathan Denton at KD's Studios, 78 Church Path, London W4 5BJ3

Published by:

Aardvark Press
P.O. Box 1176
Mesilla Park, NM 88047-1176

Tel. : (505) 526 4000

ISBN 0- 945777 - 13 -2

From Sir Alec Guinness

Anyone capable of making me sing three
notes has a sort of genius - and that goes
for John Dalby.

I'm no businessman but I would thoroughly
recommend his book to any aspiring actor; or,
indeed, to any performer who wishes to regain
his vocal skills.

It is a totally sensible, readable and
enjoyable vade-mecum for all who
need to communicate by speech.

Author's note:

John Dalby worked with Sir Alec Guinness
on the film, "A Passage to India"

T.... | This sign and the vertical line following it represents those sections that have been recorded or referred to on tape. Some of the exercises are easier to follow when heard but, to facilitate the use of the 93 minute tape, the sections should be read first.

Foreword

I have known John Dalby for many years, but I never cease being impressed anew by his immense versatility. Not only is he a gifted musician, composer and performer ... he is also an outstanding teacher of vocal techniques.

However serious he may be when discussing music, theater and the voice, he never fails to find something funny or witty to say. He is a truly attentive observer, and he listens with the same delight that he takes in performing or teaching.

I shall never forget John giving a recital of songs and anecdotes at Columbia University, to celebrate the American Bi-centennial. In the absence of a microphone, every nuance of language was clearly audible ... and greatly appreciated by a large, enthusiastic audience. His attitude, affectionate but acerbic, was perfectly reflected in his voice.

He has lectured all over the world, and audiences from India to Australia to Alabama have responded to his warmth, wit and unflappable professionalism. But perhaps his most reponsive audience is composed of his students ... from stage and screen stars to aspiring youngsters, from company directors to child prodigies.

Long ago, I suggested he write a book about his teaching methods, but he insisted: " I'm not ready yet; I keep finding new ways of doing things, of reaching people more easily." But as his work with business people expanded, he realized the need for a clear guide to speaking well in the business world.

My present work as Founder and Co-Chair of the Eleanor Roosevelt Monument Fund requires speaking before large groups and small, before foundation boards and community groups.

John Dalby's lessons have been most helpful, enabling me to concentrate on my message and feel secure about my speaking voice.

I am reminded of a period in Eleanor Roosevelt's life on which all biographers comment. Her husband's illness forced her, shy and with a high pitched voice, to make many public addresses. Franklin Roosevelt's proverbial advisor, Louis Howe, worked ceaselessly with Mrs. Roosevelt to overcome her nervous giggle and tendency to ramble on. Once she felt secure in her vocal technique, she could focus all her energy on the substance of her talk. Despite her natural handicaps, she became an effective public speaker.

All of us who meet the public, in large groups or small, in business community or in community-service situations, could benefit from John Dalby's experience and expertise.

Herbert Zohn
New York
August 1993

CONTENTS

Introduction

The world of big business and high finance used to be considered rather dull and unexciting by those outsiders not involved in acquiring at least three ulcers in it but, in the last twenty years or so, things have changed dramatically.

No longer do the skilled manipulators of the business world move silently behind the closed doors of their drab offices to clinch their deals and make their millions; in the ever-widening circles of world trade and all that that entails, they have found it expedient to come out of their shells and be more communicative. Things have smartened up. Gone are the dreary offices and boardrooms. Interior-designers, once frowned on, have swept in and transformed them into luxurious suites that are a pleasure to work in and that induce a high level of performance. Colour-co-ordination and thematic design are now an accepted part of the successful business establishment. Even the plants are chosen with care.

As for young people in business today, the opportunities are greater than ever before: companies get bigger and more complex, many of them functioning on an international level; work forces are better educated and therefore expect more from their immediate superiors; technology, while removing certain routine work, creates new demands that call for sound judgment and decision making. The customer, too, is better educated and more wised-up, and expects more for his money. Accordingly, business executives are better dressed and are more stylish, the younger ones dashing to the gym in their lunch-hours to keep the waistline in trim and to ward off the excesses of what was once considered a sedentary occupation. Only one thing seems to have been forgotten: the business executive's voice.

In business, vocal ability is no longer confined to the boardroom or making the occasional after-dinner speech. There is a whole range of new demands on the voice that were inconceivable a generation ago and it would be a mistake to assume that the voice can cope without some help and consideration; it could easily let you down at the worst possible moment or,at best, not serve you as well as it could. Certainly, one's voice should not be taken for granted that it will do what you want it to in an unfamiliar situation. Take the case of certain politicians (usually a business person wearing another coat) whose voices so irritate the listener that they lose all credence. This is not good for business!

Having a good speaking voice should now be regarded as one of the new management skills. There are, we know, courses in Public Speaking and these can be very helpful but this book is about the voice itself, and how you can explore it and improve its performance.

✳

Why the Business Executive Needs a Good Voice

From the first interview for that coveted job after leaving college the voice has an important part to play. Mumbled, indistinct answers will wreck the chances of even the most brilliant candidate while hesitancy of speech will hardly recommend itself for promotion. However it is the quality of the voice that should concern us at first; a pleasing, well placed voice can work wonders as a PR and open many doors to the possessor. The voice itself, with its many indexical features, is a clear indicator of character and therefore it is vital that it does justice to its owner.

And what of the new tasks that this voice has to perform? Business people are not professionally trained actors who can usually be relied upon to make themselves heard in front of an audience and enjoy doing it. But business people need to be able to do just that,now that modern commerce uses so many promotive techniques that are blatantly borrowed from show-biz! Let me be more specific: it is an accepted procedure in some large conglomerates for a rising young executive to formulate new management development policies which he or she is then delegated to outline to various groups in all the subsidiary companies. It is a wonderful opportunity but a daunting task. The ideas may be excellent but can they be put across in such a way as to generate enthusiasm? It is, after all, like giving a performance and the more assured the better the result. Some are lucky and are well able to rise to the occasion. Others, not so lucky but maybe just as talented, do not succeed so well.

But there are even more stressful demands on the young executive's voice than the mere presentation of well thought out policies to willing listeners. Today, he or she is more and more likely to have to appear under the full glare of the media. TV interviews and press conferences can easily take their toll of an untrained voice; the fielding of questions as opposed to following a prepared script can also be an immense strain.

The worst that can happen on these occasions is the complete loss of voice just before the big moment. Nerves can do this when one is not even aware that one is nervous. Hoarseness or an aching throat are other common symptoms of a voice labouring under stressful conditions. On the other hand, a speaker may thoroughly enjoy himself and be unaware that his audience hasn't heard a word; or the audience might have heard every word but found the voice irritating. Under these conditions an audience soon loses interest and becomes restless, and that is counter-productive.

There are those speakers, of course, who can talk a lot of bunkum but who do it with such style and conviction that the audience get carried away by it.

So we can see that it is important for the young executive to possess a voice that has carrying power without being loud; a voice that neither grates on the listener nor lulls him to sleep; a voice that is both compelling and persuasive and that does the speaker and his material justice. It is pointless to have wonderful ideas if you can't put them across to the people you want to impress. Take the case of the young television news reporter who had a remarkable facility for getting a good scoop and quickly working it into a script but who rarely got the chance to transmit her work because the management, quite justifiably, didn't approve of her high, whining voice. This caused her great anguish until she very sensibly did something about it. Now she is a familiar contributor to British television news programmes.

The human voice is part of a wonderful machine that is very much taken for granted. We learn to speak as children by copying those around us and tend to leave it at that.

What is needed to make the voice work well - and even the best voices respond to a little attention - is to examine how this wonderful machine works.

To examine each of its many parts and to make sure that each one functions as it should in the scheme of the whole machine. Then we shall get results.

Vocal Demands in Business Today

In all walks of life, people should be able to stand up and say a few words without it being an agony or an embarrassing shambles. Some individuals enjoy public speaking and can't wait to jump to their feet; others dread it and will do everything they can to avoid the possibility of making fools of themselves.

Those who can handle public speaking with ease can make all the difference to the smooth running of events and in making all those people present feel that they are part of the scheme of things. Apart from having an audible voice in the first place, the great thing is to *want* to communicate and to be informative and to give the impression that you are talking to friends. This is not always easy in some situations, especially in politics for instance, where you would undoubtedly meet with hostility and heckling. But even here, treating an adversary as a friend, even if you are putting him down, works very well and prevents one from getting ruffled.

Business people have always been able to speak with some sort of voice even if only between themselves but the vocal demands today are many and varied and increasingly so.

As yet, a computer cannot successfully give a vote of thanks or warmly introduce a new member of staff. Neither can it open an exhibition or stand in for the Best Man at a wedding. A computer cannot perform any of the speech-making skills discussed below because it lacks one vital factor - the personal touch.

THE BUSINESS PROMOTION

One of the reasons I decided to write this book was that a highly successful young business executive came to see me because he was losing his voice in a campaign to promote new policies throughout the various branches of his company.

As well as losing his voice, the young man complained of acute pains in his throat. I asked him to 'do' his promotion through, as per performance, and he obliged. At once, it was obvious to see what was wrong: his breathing was shallow and badly regulated so that his voice was in no way connected with his solar plexus or 'centre' (P. 213) with the result that all the effort was coming from his throat - hence the aching. The ideas he was promoting were good and progressive but the poor vocal performance made them seem dull, just facts and figures with little life. He seemed detached from his subject which, in a sense, he was. If he was enthusiastic about his propositions he failed to project them.

A business promotion is almost like doing a show or a recital. A great deal of preparation and assembling of ideas has to be done. Once you are satisfied that what you have to say is right you should consider how best to put it across to your audience. As well as getting your voice into good shape for the verbal onslaught, here are a few useful pointers:

  1. Decide whether or not you are going to illus-

trate your promotion with visual aids such as photographs, slides, blue-prints, graphs and/or models.

2. Decide how much you will read and how much you can do off the cuff.

3. If you are using a prepared script, go through it very slowly, one word at a time, beforehand (P. 244). This definitely instils the words into your brain.

4. Be enthusiastic about your ideas and show it; enthusiam should be infectious, of the sort that sells sand to Arabs and ice to Eskimos!

5. Don't be afraid of using your personality; remember: personality sells!

6. Don't drone on about projects just from your own point of view. This can bore an audience.

7. Keep everything brief and lively.

8. Impress your listeners but don't baffle them.

9. Keep half an ear open for your audience; if it gets restless or fidgety, liven things up a little. An amusing anecdote always helps.

10. Invite questions but make sure you are going to know the answers!

CHAIRING A MEETING

Chairing a meeting may seem a straightforward task once one has got to the dizzy heights of being a company chairman, but sometimes a meeting has to be chaired by someone other than Mr. or Mrs. Big. Vocally, there are certain demands to be met.

1. As a Chairperson, your voice should be able to control a group of disparate individuals round a board-room table or at even larger meetings.

2. You should always be audible to the person who is farthest away. From this point of view, before you begin the meeting, you should take

stock of the size of the space occupied and the number of people in it.

3. As far as audibility is concerned, small rooms can be deceptive, especially if they are full of upholstery and curtains which absorb sound, so a certain amount of projection is necessary.

4. Your voice should be firm and clear and should achieve the difficult feat of being audible to all present yet giving the impression of intimacy. Thus, everyone present is drawn into the meeting.

5. Sometimes your voice should be incisive and capable of cutting into the speaker at the end of the table who's rambling on too much.

6. At other times, your voice needs to be more coaxing or even cajoling in order to draw out the best from the more reserved people present.

It is surprising how many people with something worthwhile to contribute are nervous of speaking at meetings. An astute chairman will sense this and draw them out.

7. It hardly needs to be said that a sense of humour is invaluable for breaking the ice in what could be a stuffy meeting - a Board Meeting should not be a Bored Meeting.

8. Even the most seasoned chairperson should warm his or her voice up before a meeting, even if it's only a few whispered 'HA's'.

SPEAKING AT A MEETING

Are you one of those people who might have something worth while to contribute to a meeting but who curl up at the thought of speaking?

We all know that feeling of working oneself up into a panic, wanting to speak but terrified to do so; the holding of the breath and the thumping heart-beat, and the agonized feeling of incompetence when the meeting ends and we haven't had our say. Anyone who is used to speaking at meetings or who enjoys holding forth in public will probably never have felt like this or has forgotten what it is like but it is a very real problem for some. It may not be a vocal problem, as such, but usually the breathing is at fault, stemming possibly from timidity or the fear of being shot down. These problems need to be summarily dealt with.

1. When you are at a meeting, it is a good plan to note what other, more experienced people do and how, if they wish to speak, they 'address the chair' which simply means that their statements are directed to the chairperson and prefixed by the words, "Mr. Chairman" or "Madam Chairman".

2. Even if you wish to speak to or answer another person at the meeting, it is usually done 'through the chair'. This is a time-honoured way of defusing personal feelings. However, some meetings are less formal nowadays. Judge for your self.

3. If you have a mental block about speaking at meetings, practise the exercises on Breath into Voice (P. 82) and the Positive Voice (P. 118-119).

4. Rehearse yourself at home with imaginary statements which might begin like this: "Mr. Chairman, I agree with the last speaker but..." or "Madam Chairman, I saw this myself and I am sorry to have to say ..."

5. Practise your statements at home with as much confidence as you can muster. Even try them with some knee-bends and bouncing about on your haunches.

6. If you find you lack the courage to raise your hand in order to attract the attention of the chairperson, a good tip is to breathe well out, wait

until you feel the need to breathe in and, as you do so, raise your hand without hesitation.

7. At some larger meetings, speakers may be required to prefix their statements with their own names. It is surprising how many of us dislike saying our names out loud even when we are alone. If you are like this, do some practice on it. First of all, say a name that is not your own. Say it loud and clear several times before trying your own name. Then try saying your name, imagining it is somebody else's name. Finally, say your own name, loud and clear, *knowing* it is your name and being proud of it.

INTERVIEWING CANDIDATES FOR A JOB

It is the interviewer's task, not only to question the candidate as to his or her qualifications and suitability for the job, but to find out what sort of person the candidate is. On both sides, it is very much a vocal confrontation.

1. As an interviewer, you are in a position of great power. Remember, nothing is gained by abusing that power and putting the candidate at a disadvantage.

2. In order to draw out as much information as possible from a candidate, you should adopt a friendly manner with a warm, reassuring voice.

3. Once the candidate has acquired some confidence and has been drawn out, you should only interject in order to stimulate more information. Interrupting can make a candidate dry up.

4. It is important to listen not only to *what* is being said, but also as to *how* it is being said, for much can be revealed here that is not always intended.

5. Do not be wooed by a lovely voice or be put off by an ugly voice, but listen for clues that may

indicate what is behind the voice - honesty and
reliability or the reverse.

6. The standard of a candidate's speech may indicate the standard of his or her education, but this
is not always so.

7. It is also important to observe the general
posture of the candidate and, in particular, to
watch the hands; they are a great indication of
capability or ineptitude.

The best interviewer I ever knew was very successful at
smelling a rat by these observations of ear and eye.
Subsequent checking always proved him right. However, he was equally successful in sensing talent in
unlikely candidates which was infinitely more reward-
ing.

BEING INTERVIEWED FOR A JOB

Being interviewed for a job is something we all have to go
through at some time in our lives. It is always an ordeal
and as we get older it tends to get more humiliating so
it is essential to preserve a sense of pride. Unless a
company is desparate to have your services, the interviewer is in a very strong position. On the other hand, it
is possible that he or she is as nervous as you are. Either
way, as I said in the last section, it is very much a vocal
confrontation and it is important that you, as the
candidate, should sound at your best. It is no good being
brilliant at your work if you sound like a mouse when
you talk about it.

1. While waiting before the interview, do not hold
your breath and breathe in gulps but sit calmly
and do the panting exercise (P. 79) through your
nose to avoid drying your mouth. Alternate this
with a slow breath, through your mouth, released
on a whispered 'HA' (P. 80).

2. As you go into the interview room , breathe out fully and let the demand to breathe in take care of the rest of your breathing (P. 75)

3. Upon greeting, smile inwardly as well as outwardly, with your mouth slightly open, then speech will come easily.

4. If you are nervous, try to remember that the interviewer could be even more nervous than you are.

5. All questions that you are likely to be asked should have been mentally, if not vocally, rehearsed beforehand so that your answers are clear and not hesitant.

6. Your voice should be well modulated, giving the impression that you are at ease with the situation, so keep your breathing deep in the abdominal area.

7. When the interviewer asks a question, listen carefully and look straight into his or her eyes. If you find this difficult, look at the bridge of their nose!

8. If you have any weak spots and they are being looked for, don't let them be found.

9. Some interviewers are sympathetic and give the impression that they are really interested in you, even going so far as to make you feel that you are the only person suitable for the job. Do not be taken in by this but ask some searching questions yourself. You have the right.

10. It is important that your voice gives the best possible impression of *you*.

GIVING A LECTURE OR TALK

As far as vocal technique is concerned, there is no difference in giving a lecture or a talk. Lectures are generally recognized as being more didactic, perhaps more earnest, than talks; even so, either can be instructive and both should be entertaining. Audibility, of course, is of prime importance and all the exercises in this book are geared towards it.

1. In giving a lecture or talk, it is most important to size up the room or hall where you are to speak. Some large halls have excellent acoustics while some small rooms have bad acoustics so it is advisable to try out your venue whenever possible.

2. If you are going to have the use of a microphone, this should also be tried out beforehand.

3. A good speaker will draw a large audience into his confidence as though giving an intimate chat. This is not so easy to do with a sound-system blaring away. (See next section.)

4. The ease of giving a lecture rests mainly in knowing what you are going to say without being glued to a script or notes. Churchill said that if you use notes you should "brandish them", which rather rules out actually reading them.

5. Most speakers sensibly use a list of headings to keep them on track through a long lecture and to avoid that irritating business of leaving out something vital.

6. Using notes or headings raises the burning question as to whether to wear glasses or not. For habitual wearers, or those who don't need them at all, there is no problem but, for those who only wear glasses for reading, it is preferable not to wear them when talking to an audience. My advice is to make your list of headings large enough to read without them. If, of course, you have to read some direct quote or reference, your glasses should be put on with aplomb.

7. Always warm up your voice beforehand. Use any favourite exercise even if it's only 'MEE-MEE-MEE'. I always recommend a few whispered 'HA's' at the last minute, or a few gentle 'HUMS' but

anything is better than nothing.

8. Before you begin, take a look round at some of the faces in front of you - look pleased to see them and look eager to commence but always wait that extra second. Breathe out fully and allow the breath to replace itself before you launch into your opening remarks.

THE TELEVISION INTERVIEW

If you are going to be interviewed on television, you will most probably know what you are going to be interviewed about. Quite often the questions to be asked are discussed beforehand which makes matters easier and you can have your facts ready but this is not always so.

1. If you are nervous before the interview and waiting around a lot, do not take in gulps of air and hold your breath as this causes hyper-ventilation and a quicker heartbeat. Always breathe out as fully as you can and wait to feel the need to breathe in to settle your breathing. Some fast but silent panting (P. 79), through your nose to avoid drying your mouth, is also very helpful.

2. Before the interview begins, a few whispered 'HA's' will help to clear the airway and tone up the vocal cords, thus avoiding the ubiquitous frog in the throat that so often besets the first words spoken.

3. A jotting pad and pencil may be provided but it is advisable to take your own in case you need to make notes.

4. Keep any notes or references easily to hand.

5. Sit comfortably so that you can breath easily.

6. The interviewer may put you at your ease or he may be out to get your guts in which case, keep your breathing slow and deep, and don't get ruffled.

7. It helps if you regard the cameras and the cameramen behind them as friends to confide in.
8. Where possible, answers should begin with a firm 'yes' or 'no', followed by the relevent information.
9. With questions that begin with "How do you feel about...", it is a good thing to commence your reply with "I feel..." rather than the universal "Well..." which is meaningless and merely acts as a fulcrum. "Well..." weakens the impact and should be avoided.
10. Another word to avoid is "basically" which has become so overworked that it is meaningless. As for "You know...", always assume that people *don't* know!

THE PRESS CONFERENCE

A press conference can be either a sedate affair or it can be totally unruly, depending on who has called it and whether the topic is inflammatory or not. Either way, you will be making a statement or answering questions or both. You may be seated in the familiar comfort of your office with a few polite journalists and perhaps a camera or two or you may be in a larger area behind a phalanx of microphones under the glare of television lights and cameras.

Press conferences can be very nerve-wracking so it is essential to remain cool, calm and collected. Journalists seem to be less polite nowadays and more probing, sometimes to the point of being untactful.

1. Whether it is going to be a stormy press conference or not, be sure to get your breathing in good order before you face the firing squad. Do some fast gentle panting through your nose

followed by a few deep breaths down to your waist; hold each breath down for a few seconds and flex your abdominal muscles against your diaphragm. If you are wearing a belt, push hard against it; if you are not, imagine it. It makes you feel as strong as a boxer!

2. If you are being questioned, listen very carefully and take your time before answering. Don't be afraid of a little silence - keep them waiting.

3. Avoid making statements that could be taken in two ways or the wrong construction could be put on it; journalists are adept at twisting remarks to suit their own needs.

4. Smile whenever it is appropriate. This helps to diffuse any tension you may have and besides, you will look better.

5. However loquacious you may feel, don't say one word more than is necessary.

MICROPHONE TECHNIQUE

Many public speakers today are pampered with microphones which often prevent them not only from projecting their voices but also their personalities as well. A microphone may make a voice louder but it also magnifies the faults in a voice, sometimes distorting them to the point of unintelligibility. This is frustrating for the audience but even more for the speaker who is no longer self-reliant but at the mercy of technology.

Microphones like some voices and not others; a well-focused, resonant voice will be picked up even at some distance while a badly produced voice fails to register however near it is to the microphone.

For all the modern audio-technology available today, microphone technique is still something that deserves some attention. The old days of having to beware of "bumping" the mike with over-plosive 'B's' and 'P's' may have passed but there are other things to consider.

1. Always try out the microphone and sound-system beforehand - and get someone to listen. It is well worth the trouble and sets your mind at rest.

2. It is unlikely that you will need to use a microphone in the distinctly personal way that popular singers or stand-up comedians do but a few lessons can be learnt.

3. The microphone is the modern singer's best friend for without it many of them would be without a marketable voice. They know how to use the mike, how close to be for the intimate phrases and how far back to get when they are going to 'let rip'.

4. If you have a stand-mike in front of you make sure the position is right in relationship to your face, preferably lower than your chin; you don't want to feel you daren't move your head.

5. Familiarize yourself with the mike so that you can gauge your distance - closer for the quiet passages and back a bit for something louder; it works wonders on an audience instead of the usual uniformity of amplified sound that drones on and sends everyone to sleep.

6. The modern chest mike - almost a badge of office on TV chat shows - is a remarkable piece of technology that clips conveniently onto a tie or a lapel but can be a problem with a low-cut dress! A certain amount of intimate wiring also has to be hidden in your clothes by the sound engineer's assistant but this can be quite fun. Once on and working, you must remember not to bang the mike in moments of enthusiasm or an earth-quake will reverberate through the building.

Chest mikes are usually controlled by sound engineers who know when to switch you off, but beware of this. There was the notorious occasion when a famous musical comedy star had just made her exit to thunderous applause and went straight to the lavatory (or bathroom). She had not been switched off and the audience was treated to a variety of sounds including the theatre's plumbing. The moral is that microphones should be treated with respect and caution!

TELEPHONE TECHNIQUE

Telephone technique is similar to microphone technique and, indeed, many of the same points apply. The telephone is very much taken for granted but I think it is safe to say that more business is conducted on it than off it. Allright, it is irritating to get phone calls in the middle of, say, making an important decision, but that very call could be instrumental in helping you make that decision. On the other hand, for the caller, it is off-putting to be greeted with a terse or hostile "Yes?"

1. It is a good idea to give your throat a quick preparation every time you pick the telephone up. It soon becomes a habit. A couple of "a-hems" with your lips closed will suffice.
2. High-pitched voices are not so successful on the telephone as those that are lower pitched and a *loud* high-pitched voice is excruciating at the receiving end. How often have you held the receiver at arm's length and still been able to hear what is said? It may be an achievement but it's not good for business.
3. If your voice is high and squeaky it needs to be lowered for reasons other than just the telephone.
4. Sometimes one is in the strong position on the

telephone, sometimes the weak. If you are in the weak position, say for example, ringing up a Very Important Person for an interview, you will probably be nervous. To avoid hesitations or mumbling, write out a little script for yourself before ringing then, while you are dialling, do some fast gentle panting to loosen up your breathing. *Don't* do anything like whispered 'HA's' or you may sound like the Heavy Breather on the line!

5. Your powers of persuasion are possibly at their most effective when aimed at a receiver so near to someone's brain - or, for that matter, their heart. Whichever you want to aim at.

Different Types of Voices (Which is Yours?)

Every voice has an individual quality that distinguishes it from all others. No two voices are the same; like faces, they can be similar but not identical. This is partly due to the physical shape of various parts of the vocal mechanism, such as the larynx, the pharynx and the resonating cavities, and partly due to the particular way the voice is used or mis-used. It would be interesting to see at this stage if you can identify your own vocal characteristics among those listed below.

Voice Qualities
smooth, rough, warm, cold, high-pitched, low-pitched, soft, hard, melodious, flat, mellow, harsh, fruity, hollow, husky, tremulous, raucous, etc.

Allied to the voice qualities and the different ways that people use their voices are the modes of speech. It is these qualities and modes that enable us to recognize the voices of people we know.

Modes of Speech
quick, slow, precise, slovenly, clipped, slurred, forthright, hesitant, monotonous, over-inflected, downward-inflected, upward-inflected, etc.

On top of the voice qualities and the modes of speech,

the voice can be affected temporarily and sometimes
permanently by various physical states.

Physical States That Affect the Voice
fatigue, pain, catarrh, nerves, shock,
inflammation (bronchitis, laryngitis,
pharyngitis and sinusitis), asthma,
tuberculosis, dyspnoea (shortness of
breath), cold (shivering), hot (puffing),
alcohol, drugs, swollen adenoids,
cleft-palate, missing teeth, badly fitting
dentures, etc.

Feelings and emotions also affect the voice but usually only temporarily.

Feelings and Emotions that Affect the Voice
happiness, misery, ecstasy, grief, shyness,
fright, hatred, love, nervousness, worry,
anger, amusement, contempt, sympathy,
slyness, spirituality, lust, satisfaction,
depression, anxiety, hysteria - from joy or
from grief, etc.

Some of the above descriptions could be regarded as
faults but most of them are not, though they may *cause*
faultiness.

❋

Some Common Faults

The faults listed below are mostly due to mis-use of one or more parts of the vocal mechanism:

> breathy voice, croaky voice, voice pitched too high, voice pitched too low, "pulpit tenor", "adenoidal" sounding, nasal sounding, tight jaw, over-use of jaw, "frozen" lips, constant rounding of lips, constant spreading of lips, lazy tongue, lazy 'R', over-sibilance (hissing).

Breathy voice - caused by faulty phonation where some air is vibrated into vocal tone and the rest escapes unvibrated.
Solution: Work through Efficient Phonation (P. 88) and all the Resonance section (P. 100).
Croaky voice - similar to breathy voice only worse. The sound seems to be scraping the throat. Little or no resonance.
Solution: Work through Efficient Phonation (P. 88) and all the Resonance section (P. 100).
Voice pitched too high - caused by tension in various places which are sometimes difficult to pin-point as the fundamental cause can be psychological.
Solution: Work through Loosening Your Throat Mus-

cles (P. 72), Finding Your Own Pitch (P. 92)
and Pitch Exercises (P. 208)

Voice pitched too low - caused by too much slack-
ness where some tension is required. Again,
the cause can be psychological, trying to hide
or smother the voice.

Solution: Work through Finding Your Own Pitch
(P. 92) and Pitch Exercises (P. 208).

"Pulpit tenor" - caused by constant raising of
the larynx which in turn tightens the back of
the tongue and other surrounding muscles. A
tight larynx is a deep, ingrained habit that
is hard to break. I call it the "clenched fist"
larynx because that is exactly what it feels
like.

Solution: Gradually break down the tension by
working through Loosening Your Neck, Jaw
and Shoulders (P. 69), Loosening Your Throat
Muscles (P. 72), Exploring the Bottom of Your
Voice (P. 102),
Tongue Awareness (P. 142) and Tongue
Looseners (P. 143).

"Adenoidal" voice - assuming the adenoids are
not swollen, this is caused by the constant
raising of the soft palate so that there is no
nasal resonance.

Solution: Work through all the humming exercises
(P.107-P.113), the 'Pinched EE' (P. 114), Nasa-
lizing and Oralizing (P. 117) and Soft Palate
Awareness (P. 149)

Nasal voice - caused by the constant dropping of
the soft palate onto the back of the tongue so
that there is little or no oral resonance.

Solution: Same as for the "Adenoidal" voice as
a balance needs to be found between the two.

Tight jaw - very common. So many people seem to rely
on this tension. Either the upper and lower
teeth are clamped together or the jaw is

thrust forward or pulled back. The jaw is very obstinate in letting go.

Solution: Work on Loosening Your Jaw, Neck and Shoulders (P. 69), Jaw Awareness (P. 137), Letting Go of Your Jaw (P. 138) and Jaw Looseners (P. 139). Also Tongue Looseners (P. 143) will help separate the jaw from the tongue.

Over-use of jaw - the "chomping" look. This cuts words up because the jaw is doing half the work of the tongue. It is also extremely tiring, both for the speaker and for anyone watching.

Solution: Same as for the other jaw problems, especially Jaw Awareness (P. 137) and Tongue Looseners (P. 143).

"Frozen" lips - where the lips never move - and not much else, either. The effect is like a corpse speaking or someone who has just been injected by the dentist.

Solution: Work through Letting Go of Your Jaw (P. 138), Lip Awareness (P. 157) and Lip Looseners (P. 158)

Constant rounding of lips - similar to "frozen" lips but more pronounced. It gives a too precious and proper sound to speech.

Solution: Same as for "frozen" lips.

Constant spreading of lips - speaking with a fixed smile. This distorts speech in another way, making it sound insincere or cunning.

Solution: Same as for "frozen" lips. The right balance needs to be found between the spread and rounded positions.

Lazy tongue - where the tongue hardly moves, causing a general indistinctness. Sometimes the tongue is downright inert or it leaves a lot of the work to the jaw. Sometimes the tongue is too tense to move efficiently.

Solution: Work through Loosening Your Jaw,

Neck and Shoulders (P. 69), Letting Go of Your Jaw (P. 138), Tongue Awareness (P. 142) and Tongue Looseners (P. 143).

Lazy 'R' - similar to lazy tongue but more complicated.

Solution: See How to Cure a 'Lazy R' (P. 164).

Over-sibilance - caused by faulty position tongue and sometimes of the jaw as well.

Solution: See How to Cure a Hissing 'S' (P. 169) and How to Cure sibilant 'T's' and 'D's' (P. 174).

NOTE: It is good to pinpoint problems and to work at their solution but do remember that all parts of the vocal mechanism are inter-connected and that problems should be worked on with that in mind.

The human voice is part of a wonderful machine that is very much taken for granted. We learn to speak as children by copying those around us and tend to leave it at that.

What is needed to make the voice work well - and even the best voices respond to a little attention - is to examine how this wonderful machine operates.

We need to examine each of its many parts and to make sure that each one functions as it should in the scheme of the whole machine. Then we shall get results.

❋

The Vocal Mechanism

The vocal mechanism is like a highly complex musical instrument in which there are many interlinking components. Put into simple terms and continuing the musical instrument analogy, these components can be divided into four sections: the Bellows, the Reed, the Articulators and the Resonators.

The Bellows, needless to say, are concerned with blowing air through the instrument in much the same way as the bellows of the old pipe-organ. Without air no vocal sound can be made. Included in this section are the lungs, the diaphragm, the abdominal muscles, the ribs and the muscles between the ribs (intercostals) and the wind-pipe. At the top of the wind-pipe is the reed, the only section with a single component namely, the larynx or voice-box, which produces the notes. Without this vital piece of equipment no vocal sound can be made either. The rest of the musical instrument is concerned with enhancing the sound that the Bellows and the Reed have made. The Articulators, mostly contained in the mouth, formulate this sound into something more specific, such as words, while the Resonators, which are mostly in the nasal area, amplify it and project it towards the Receiver - in other words, somebody's ear.

Here is a list of the main components of the vocal mechanism beginning at its lowest point which, as will be seen later, corresponds more or less to the order of use when producing a sound.

The diaphragm
The abdominal muscles
The ribs and chest
The lungs
The windpipe
The larynx or voice-box
The throat or pharynx
The jaw
The tongue
The soft palate
The hard palate
The teeth
The lips
The nasal cavity
The nose
The nasal sinuses
The frontal sinuses
The top of the skull

Nearly all these components, as we shall see, have a far more fundamental use but, when they are engaged in making vocal sound, for maximum efficiency, each component should work in perfect conjunction with the others.

If the sound is poor, it means that one or more of the components is not in the right place at the right time, or is being misused or not used at all. This being so, I think it would be worthwhile to examine each component separately or with its neighbour to see if and how it works. A brief look at the spine precedes this.

THE SPINE

The spine is part of the vocal mechanism in so far as it is the frame which supports and holds everything together. It is important that it should be allowed to do this as efficiently as possible. A slumped, twisted or bent spine will naturally impair good vocal sound.

The spine, together with the back, provides an important resonator - like a back wall to bounce your voice off. You may have noticed, when you're having a friendly conversation with someone and you've put your arm round their shoulder, very distinct vibrations coming through their back when they speak, particularly in the lower register.

If you haven't experienced this, then I suggest you try it. You'll make a lot of friends, and that can't be bad for business.

THE DIAPHRAGM AND THE ABDOMINAL MUSCLES

The diaphragm is a dome-shaped muscular partition which separates the thoracic and abdominal cavities. It is attached all round to the bottom of the rib-cage rather like a trampoline. In the middle of it is a small aperture (hiatus) through which the oesophagus and aorta pass. The main function of the diaphragm is its domination of the mechanics of breathing. In breathing, the nerve impulses stimulate the diaphragm to contract, causing it to flatten out. As this happens the lungs expand causing air to rush into them. When the diaphragm relaxes it reverts to its domed shape and pushes the air out of the lungs again. Some people are under the misapprehension that the diaphragm is situated in front of their abdomen where its movement is most evident so it is well to keep the trampoline image in mind, the back and sides being equally important.

Similarly, in considering the abdominal muscles which form a strong wall over the front of the body from the ribs downwards, attention should be given to the muscles round the sides and back. Taken as a whole, they are like a wide, tough, elastic girdle right around the waist. It is essential that this girdle should work in conjunction with the movements of the diaphragm. For vocal purposes they should work sometimes *with* the diaphragm, sometimes *against*. I shall give plenty of examples of this, later on.

THE LUNGS

The lungs are the real bellows of the respiratory and vocal systems. They are like two sponge-filled bags and, together with the heart, they fill the chest cavity. At the top they are pointed and extend a little above the line of the collar bones; at the bottom they are wide and rest on the diaphragm. The prime function of the lungs is to supply the blood with oxygen without which we could not live. By some miraculous osmosis they can extract the oxygen from inhaled air and pass it into the bloodstream; at the same time they can eject carbon dioxide (which can be likened to industrial waste) from the blood into the air that is to be exhaled and thus got rid of. A small amount of oxygen is exhaled with the carbon dioxide just as a small amount of carbon-dioxide is left in the blood. It is this small amount of carbon-dioxide that stimulates the brain to repeat its messages to the diaphragm and the intercostal muscles to breathe in again for the further supply of oxygen. And so it goes on through life.

The respiratory system is a marvellously efficient machine and should be respected as such and it is a sobering thought that our lives depend on this interchange of gases. However, it is the gas that is expelled from our lungs (the waste) that concerns us. It is that gas that we use for speaking or singing.

The word, lung, comes from the Greek word meaning 'light' (in weight). It is well for us to keep that feeling of lightness and buoyancy beneath our ribs.

THE CHEST

The chest consists of a bony cage formed by the ribs, the sternum (breastbone) and thoracic vertebrae. It protects the heart and the lungs. Between the ribs are two layers of intercostal muscles, wonderful web-like structures which govern the flexibility of the cage to allow for the expansion and contraction of the lungs as they breathe in and out. No one is quite sure how much the intercostal muscles anticipate the movement of the lungs but, for vocal purposes, it is best to assume that they act passively and *allow* the expansion as and when the breath is taken in and that they fall gently back into place when you breathe out. This would certainly seem to be the case when we are asleep. The idea that the ribcage has to be lifted in order to breathe in is misleading. Doing it consciously will cause a great deal of unnecessary tension.

THE WINDPIPE

The windpipe (trachea) is exactly what it says it is - a pipe that carries wind (or air) to and from the lungs. It, too, is remarkably constructed, being composed of fibro-elastic tissue in which incomplete rings of cartilege are embedded to keep the pipe from collapsing. At the top end it is attached to the underside of the larynx. The lower end divides into two tubes, the left bronchus and the right bronchus. (We become aware of the bronchi when we suffer from bronchitis.) Each bronchus enters a lung where it branches like a tree into ever smaller tubes that take the air to and from the lungs where the osmosis takes place. This simplified description is sufficient for our purposes here.

The windpipe doesn't actually *do* anything, it simply serves as an airway. Care should be taken to keep it free from obstruction and to keep it as elongated as possible. Pulling the neck into the shoulders can cause the top rings to become compressed and the voice to sound strangulated. Lengthening the spine and extending the neck will help to prevent this.

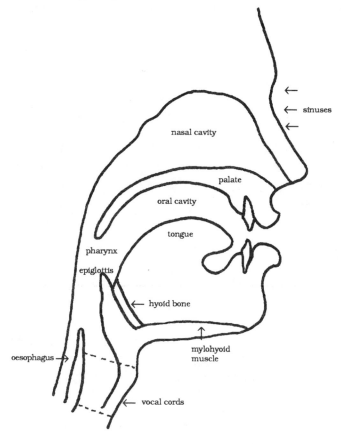

Figure 1: The Upper Vocal Mechanism

THE LARYNX

The larynx, situated at the top of the windpipe, is a trian-
gular-shaped structure of cartilage and muscle containing the vocal cords.It is surmounted by a leaf-shaped lid,
called the epiglottis, which closes like a trap-door when
we swallow. Indeed, one of the prime functions of the
larynx is to prevent food or liquid from entering the
windpipe; without this involuntary closure the lungs
would become full of foreign bodies and we would
suffocate. We all know what it's like when something
goes down the "wrong way" - through carelessness or
talking while eating and swallowing - and we have to
cough it up before we choke.

The vocal cords (or vocal folds) extend horizontally from
the front to the back of the larynx like a pair of muscular
elastic bands. When brought together edge to edge they
can convert the upward flow of air into sound vibrations.
Musically speaking, they are the reed of the vocal system
but, like violin or guitar strings, they can be stretched or
loosened to produce different pitches. The volume of the
sound depends on how much air is being pushed
through them.

The front extremities of the vocal cords are attached
adjacently to the inner side of the thyroid cartilage which
forms a hard point and is readily visible at the front of
a man's throat just above the collar. This perhaps
explains its popular name, Adam's apple. Eve's apple,
for reasons best known to evolution, and the fact that it
is smaller than Adam's, is hardly visible at all.

The other ends of the vocal cords are connected to two
complex groups of muscles called the arytenoids which,
with a remarkable swivel action, can cause them to
come together. In their relaxed state they are apart,
making a V-shaped opening known as the glottis; the

tiniest effort of the arytenoids brings them together, which is what we do every time we speak.

Out of the numerous states of the glottis, there are four noteworthy positions to consider:

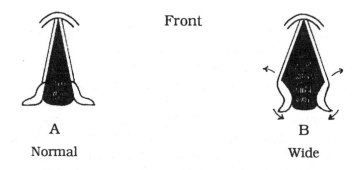

Figure 2: The Larynx

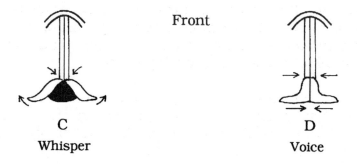

A is the relaxed position for normal breathing, B is more open for deep breathing, C is partially closed which produces a whisper, and D is the closed position which produces voice.

Mostly we use our vocal cords without any conscious thought and there is little or no sensation to differentiate between these positions apart from the results of whispering and speaking. This makes it difficult to monitor what we are actually doing. The mental concept is what dictates the final result. After that we can only sense what are doing and rely on audio-feedback to know if we have succeeded or not.

THE PHARYNX

Once above the larynx, we leave the bellows and reed for the three echo-chambers, before finally reaching the articulators and the resonators. The first of these echo-chambers is the pharynx, the space immediately above the larynx which in turn branches into the other two echo-chambers, the oral cavity, or mouth, culminating in the lips, and the nasal cavity culminating in the nose. Primarily, the pharynx is a common passage way for air going to and from the larynx and for food entering the oesophagus. However, the presence of food or liquid stimulates a reflex contraction of the pharyngeal tube which closes off the nasal cavity and the larynx in order to swallow. It is important to know this because the act of swallowing is in all ways contrary to the act of voca- lising. In other words, you should not speak while you are swallowing or swallow while you speak.

As an echo-chamber, the pharynx is the first enhancer of the fundamental vocal tone emitted by the vocal cords. Indeed, it is the size of the pharynx that deter- mines whether a singer has a beautiful voice or not. In plain terms, the bigger it is the better. Unfortunately, there is not much we can do to make it bigger than it already is which is why a great singing voice can rightly be described as 'God-given'. However, there is much we can do *not* to make the pharynx any *smaller* than it is. As an airway of almost fixed proportions, it can be divided into two sections by raising the soft-palate (the flexible back section of the roof of the mouth) so high that it cuts off the entire upper half — a great loss. This upper half is known as the naso-pharynx because it opens into the nasal cavity. The lower half is known as the oro-pharynx because it opens into the mouth. Here, to keep the space as big as possible, care should be taken not to raise the larynx with tension but to keep it as relaxed and low as possible. Further care should be taken to avoid pulling in the jaw or tongue as this again reduces the size of the pharynx and severely impairs vocal performance.

There is not a great deal one can do to exercise the pharynx, but I am a great believer in the power of thought — thinking it is bigger than it is and feeling that you can balloon it out while keeping it loose, helps to increase the vocal vibrations. In this way you can feel the yawn position without actually yawning, you can lift the soft palate without blocking off the nasal areas and you can avoid pulling in the jaw and the tongue. All this could be described as opening the throat.

THE ORAL CAVITY

The oral cavity or mouth is lined with mucus membrane and contains the tongue, the teeth and the salivary glands. Hence it is always moist, or should be. Its domed roof is known as the hard palate behind which is the soft palate.Of the three echo-chambers or cavities it is the most important because it is the most variable in shape, due to the immense mobility of the lower jaw and to the lips and because it contains all the equipment for transforming basic vocal sound into words. Central to this is the tongue which lies along the floor of the mouth, the floor being the jaw. One of the major tasks for clarity of speech is to separate the activity of the tongue from the jaw. Being closely connected at the back it is virtually impossible to move the jaw without the tongue moving with it, but it is perfectly possible, and indeed vital, to be able to move the tongue independently of the jaw. This will be explored in the Diction and Articulation section.

THE JAW

The jaw is the only movable part of the skull and its primary function, armed as it is with teeth, is to bite and chew food. When speaking, the jaw should be less active, for words should not be bitten or chewed. However, a lot of biting and chewing does go on when eating is not taking place, making the jaw a notorious repository of tension. Gritting the teeth is one example.

In the vocal scheme of things the jaw forms the base of the articulation mechanism, so it is important that it is in its right place, which I will explain later. It should be as free of tension as possible to allow maximum mobility; a mobility that should barely be visible.

THE TONGUE

Although we tend to think of the tongue as being in the mouth, the back of it actually extends down the front of the throat where, just above the larynx, its root is attached to the hyoid bone. This small bone, sometimes referred to as the tongue-bone, is the only bone in the body that is not part of the skeletal system. While difficult to locate, it is something that needs to be watched when speaking or singing because tension in the tongue or in the surrounding swallowing muscles will depress the hyoid bone onto the larynx causing it to buckle and in turn compress the top of the trachea, making the voice strangled and croaky. Even if this isn't a bad habit it often happens to people when they are nervous.

The prime function of the tongue, of course, is to give us the sensation of taste and to push the food around the mouth so that it gets properly chewed in readiness for swallowing. But, as an organ of speech, it has the greatest responsibility in transforming pure vocal tone into actual words. Not for nothing is the word 'tongue' synonymous with language. Its complex muscular struc- ture makes it a virtuoso in the mouth where it is capable of assuming a great variety of positions necessary to speech. Able to adapt into many shapes, it can shrink itself smaller or extend itself well beyond its original form as, for instance, when pushed out over the front teeth. Yet, in spite of its considerable flexibility or, perhaps because of it, the tongue is a surprisingly disobedient organ.

In speech, the tongue has a distinct position, sometimes minutely so, for every segment of every word. Sometimes it has to flick about quickly and quite often it doesn't get there in time and the word is blurred. Of course, many of us have no idea where the tongue should be for the various parts of words, having learnt speech on an entirely imitative basis.

When the doctor asks a child to open his mouth and say 'Ah', he is pretty confident that in doing so the child's tongue will depress at the back so that he can see down the throat. (It doesn't always work!) It is unlikely that the doctor will ask the child just to flatten the back of his tongue, because the child has no conscious control of it. That the tongue seems to have a will of its own is a common complaint and is good reason for making ourselves more aware of it in order to control it.

The tongue is remarkably like an untrained hand on the piano; each finger is perfectly capable of pressing down any key it happens to be on. Getting to the right key at the right time requires a great deal of awareness and practice. The same goes for the tongue. Most of us can manage the tip of it quite well and run it round our teeth with ease but, as soon as vocalisation takes place, the thing tends to stiffen and bunch up. This is usually caused by tension at the back near the hyoid bone and the larynx. Freeing the back of the tongue and separating its activity from the larynx and throat immediately improves the voice. It is like loosening the wrist of a pianist so that the fingers are free to perform.

Of the several sub-lingual muscles connected to the tongue there is one that needs to be watched. This is the mylohyoid which is attached to the hyoid bone and extends underneath to the tip of the chin. This is easy to locate by pressing your thumb under your chin just in front of your throat where there is a V-shaped space in your jaw bone. If this is hard then you're in trouble! It is a prime interferer; even if it is soft in repose it frequently stiffens up at the merest hint of vocalization. Undoing that stiffness is a major task which many of the tongue loosening exercises will help to achieve. It will certainly help to separate the tongue from the jaw.

THE ROOF OF THE MOUTH OR PALATE

The roof of the mouth is generally referred to as the palate, both hard and soft, the hard palate being the more readily discernible, against which, as children, we

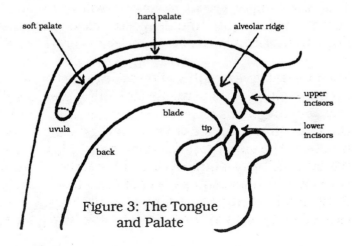

Figure 3: The Tongue
and Palate

could make those astonishingly loud and satisfying clicks with our tongues. Behind it, the soft palate is, of course, a continuation of the hard palate. It is only soft because the palatal bone does not reach so far back and because the membrane is left loosely stretched across the pharynx like an awning or piece of umbrella.

Although we tend to think of the palate as being in these two sections, for the purposes of speech it is more convenient to think of it in three: the soft palate at the back, the high domed roof of the hard palate in the middle, and the alveolar ridge, the bony prominence behind the top, front teeth.

Without the palate and alveolar ridge, few words as we know them could be pronounced properly, if at all, for it is against them that the tongue wields its remarkable dexterity in the formation of words. Further enhancement can be effected with the teeth, lips and cheeks but it is the relationship between the tongue and the various parts of the palate that is most vital to the formation and articulation of speech.

The soft palate, as we have seen, can block off or open up the top of the pharynx and its position crucially affects the upper resonance of the voice. By lifting it too high, nearly all the nasal resonance is eliminated and the voice sounds dull as when one has a bad cold. In particular, the two nasal consonants 'N', 'M' and, to a certain extent, 'L' will fail to register, so that a phrase like 'Monday morning' will sound more like 'Buddy bordig'.

On the other hand, by dropping the soft palate onto the back of the tongue, nearly all the oral resonance is eliminated, reducing the voice to a thin, nasal whine. For a voice to sound clear and, at the same time pleasant, it is essential that there should be a fine balance of oral and nasal resonance. That some people are more nasal than others is a matter of personal distinction and it can be very attractive. American English is certainly more nasal than British English, which is part of its charm whereas nasalized British English is less appealing.

One more important point about the hard palate is that when it is vibrating, it can send reverberations up into the nasal cavity, of which it is the floor, and upwards and forwards into the nasal sinuses and skull.

This is what makes the voice *carry*, without effort, in large rooms and small.

THE TEETH

It need hardly be said that teeth are situated in the mouth for the purpose of tearing, biting and chewing and it is the movement of the lower jaw that energises this. As far as speech is concerned, the teeth don't actually *do* anything; they are passive articulators and serve as a foil to the tongue. Mainly, this involves the upper incisors, the lower teeth merely providing a foil for the upper lip in the sounds made by 'F' and 'Z' and an anchorage for the tip of the tongue. However, the lower teeth are indispensable for helping us measure distances from the upper teeth when lowering the jaw for certain sounds. In this, no firm rule can be applied as everyone's mouth is different. Some people have long teeth and short gums while others have short teeth and long gums, and so on. The correct dimensions have to be found for each individual.

THE LIPS

The lips are the front door of the mouth and their shape and position can greatly enhance (or spoil) the facial expression. In considering the lips, we must also consider the whole of the circular muscle that surrounds the mouth (attractively named the obicularis oris) to which the lips form a pleasant, pink edge. Extremely flexible, they can adapt themselves to many different shapes, from smiling to whistling. As with the nostrils, the mucus membrane commences just inside the lips and continues throughout the whole of the vocal and respiratory systems.

Having countless nerve endings just below the surface, the lips are extremely sensitive and can rightly be described as one of the erogenous zones. We all use them for kissing, be it a peck on the cheek or something more sensual. They are pleasure lovers, they like sipping delicious drinks. They can, and do, make signs.

But lips can also suffer; they can get bitten when their owners are upset or angry. And lips can reveal many covert things about the person within. Next to the eyes, lips can tell us more about a person's character than anything else.

We all know the tight-lipped look, or the sneer, or the inane grin, or the tell-tale trembling bottom lip when somebody is close to tears. Then there is the stiff upper lip, allegedly typical of the British, that is supposed to conceal inner feelings. Needless to say, all these states have an effect on speaking.

In speech, the lips contribute enormously to the formation and enhancement of words. Sometimes they need to be out of the way as in 'AH', or they need to be closely rounded as in 'OO'. For this to happen successfully they need to be in a complete state of freedom and any unwanted tension eliminated.

THE NASAL CAVITY

The nasal cavity is the largest of the three echo-chambers. Together with the nose and the facial sinuses, the resonance capability of this area is similar to a bank of highly sensitive loud-speakers.

The main nasal cavity itself, lined as it is with mucous membrane, is part of the airway which serves to warm and moisten air as it is inhaled. Within it are the protective reflexes of sneezing and the olfactory receptors that provide the sense of smell.

As a resonance chamber for the voice, the nasal cavity is like the body of a violin, being of fixed dimensions and shape. It is far larger than the oral cavity and its bony, ledged surface causes vocal vibrations to reverberate with greater frequency, thus creating more upper partials and harmonics which add up to a rich sonority.

The floor of the nasal cavity is the roof of the mouth and a great deal of resonance can come up through the hard palate into the 'cathedral' above. Like so many cathedrals, the nasal cavity divides into two openings at the front. These openings, divided by a thin, vertical wall of bone known as the septum, become the nostrils of the nose.

There is nothing one can 'do' to the nasal cavity other than to keep it open and to use it. In order to experience the amplitude it can give to the voice, one has only to close one's lips and hum. This is one way of ensuring that the soft palate is not blocking off the nasal cavity by being raised too high. However, most people are not very efficient at humming — there is more to it than making a noise with closed lips. This will be fully explored in the section on Resonance.

THE NOSE

The nose is generally considered first in the matter of breathing but I have left it almost to the last because, backed up as it is by the facial resonators, it is the last outpost of the voice before it travels across space in the form of sound waves to the receptors - people's ears.

The nose is like the prow of a ship; it leads us along the paths we mean to take and points the voice in the right direction.

In humans, the nose is a remarkable construction consisting of two air-vents, called nostrils, which are raised from a relatively flat face by a strut of bone and gristle. Like the nasal cavity, the nostrils are lined with mucous membrane which begins the task of warming and moistening the inhaled air, the numerous blood vessels just below the surface providing the warmth.

The hairs round the front of the nostril openings are there as filters to prevent dust, flies and other nasties from entering. Needless to say, it is important to keep these airways as clear as possible at all times, especially when vocalising. A handkerchief of some kind should always be to hand.

It may surprise you to know that you can actually exercise the nose muscles. If you watch some people you may notice that they half close their nostrils either when they breathe in or when they speak. How much better to flare your nostrils like a horse. Try it.

THE FACIAL SINUSES

The facial sinuses are small rounded cavities in the skull which have an amazing capacity for amplifying the voice far beyond its fundamental level. There are four pairs of these sinuses (Figure 4); each is lined with mucous membrane and they all drain through small ducts into the main nasal cavity. This inter-connection underlines the fact that, together, they make a formidable resonating unit.

The old Italian singing professor who said to his pupils, "You musta singa wiz zee eyes!" was right. He might equally have urged that they should speak with their eyes.

Between the eyes and between the bridge of the nose and the nasal cavity there is a honeycomb section of bone known as the ethmoidal sinuses. These are the least familiar of the four pairs of sinuses, and it is as well to acquaint ourselves with their existence because, mentally, so much can be done to open them up to receive and enhance vocal vibrations.

Most commonly known are the maxillary sinuses, and anyone who suffers from sinusitis doesn't need to be told where they are! Situated either side of the nose and extending from just under the eye sockets to just above the top teeth, they are the largest of the four pairs and the most obvious of the resonators. They are also the most vulnerable to infection and can be very painful when inflamed.

When blocked, the maxillary sinuses deaden the voice considerably.

Just above the maxillary sinuses, on either side of the actual nose-bone, are the sphenoidal sinuses. They are quite small and are situated partly in front of the ethmoidals so that the top of the nose is potentially very vibrant and resonant.

Lastly, there are the frontal sinuses, so-named because

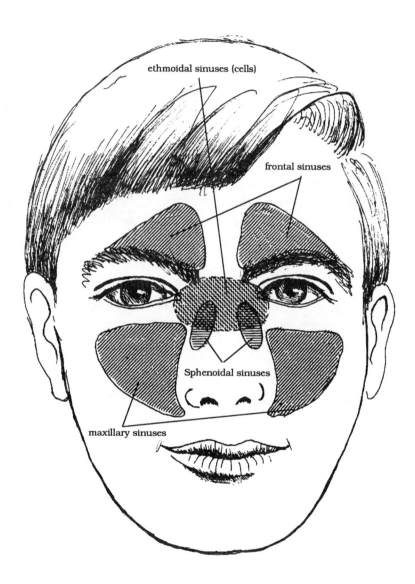

Figure 4: The Facial Sinuses

they are situated in the frontal bone of the skull, just behind the middle of the eyebrows.

THE SKULL

Depending on the looseness and freedom of the muscles governing the head, the whole of the top of the skull becomes a resonator, particularly of the higher frequencies. You can feel this quite easily by placing the palm of your hand on top of your head and alternating some low and high, short hums. You will feel some vibration on the lower sounds but very much more on the higher sounds. If you place your hand on top of someone's head while they are speaking you will be surprised how much vibration you feel.

Posture

Now that we have a clear picture of the complete vocal mechanism, let us return our attention to the spine and the subject of posture.

Good posture puts the vocal mechanism into an ideal state for performance, whereas bad posture can wreck an otherwise excellent voice. It is a waste of time to try to exercise the voice unless the posture is right.

Ever since homo sapiens stood on two legs instead of four he has had trouble with his spine, thereby giving legions of osteopaths and chiropractors a very profitable living. Back problems are usually the result of bad posture over a long period of time. Not always noticeable in young people, because of their constant mobility, it is more evident in the elderly, by which time it is accepted as the inevitable process of growing old.

In particular, I refer to the dropping forward of the top of the spine causing the back of the neck to cave in and the jaw to jut forward. In older women, this is cruelly referred to as the Dowagers' Hump but it can apply equally to men and the effect on the voice is to make it sound old and stringy. However, one does not have to be old for this dropping forward of the top of the spine to happen. Laziness or the cool laid-back attitude can be one factor; the macho gorilla stance, favoured by some young males, can be another. But mostly it is the result of occupational hazard. Crouching over a desk or telephone for hours can cause crippling problems in the neck.

The Japanese have the right idea when they encourage their workers, especially sedentary workers, to pause in their work at regular intervals to do a few breathing and physical exercises. It has been proved that the time lost is more than made up for in performance. The most exercise you will see in the majority of Western offices is a rather vulgar stretching up of the arms often coupled with a yawn. Unless it is company policy, not many individuals, particularly in communal offices, have the courage to get up from their desks occasionally and do a little stretching, loosening and deep breathing.

Lying flat on the floor is a wonderful way of getting rid of kinks in the spine and of increasing the flow of oxygen to the brain. This could be vital before making important decisions. Yet, most secretaries would get quite a shock if they came into their boss's office and found him or her flat out on the carpet (preferably with a slim book to cushion the head) despite the fact that, by so doing, they could be clearing their brain and warding off that impending coronary. No joking.

Correct posture is important but it is also difficult to define because it is not a fixed entity and should never be rigidly held. Freedom and mobility are essential. There are different postures for playing golf as there are for playing the violin or using a word-processor but they should not be immovable. The spine governs all posture and it deserves some attention. Sitting or standing up straight may sound like a good idea but it is neither comfortable nor is it, in fact, possible. Our spines are naturally curved, some more than others, rather like an elongated 'S', and the more elongated, the better. At the same time the back should be felt to be widening as advocated in Alexander Technique (see P.193).

IMPROVING YOUR SITTING POSTURE

When working, sit on a good firm chair with your knees and feet loosely apart and your shoulders and arms hanging free. Make sure your weight is evenly distributed between your ischial tuberosities — the parts of the pelvis you sit on.

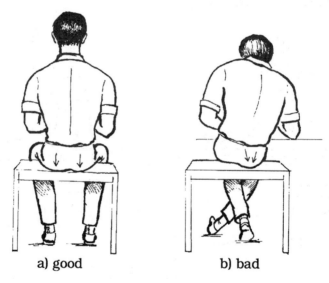

a) good   b) bad

Figure 5: Sitting Postions

Use odd moments when not concentrating on important issues to let your spine 'grow' and your back widen. Tiresome phone calls provide an ideal opportunity.

> ▪ Picture your spine as a pile of cotton reels (vertebrae) threaded onto a cord (the spinal cord) with circular pads (intervertebral discs) between each cotton reel.

- Looking straight ahead of you, let your spine lengthen upwards by imagining that you are inflating the pads between the cotton reels. Begin at the base of your spine and work slowly up. At the same time feel your back widening and let your neck flow upwards and slightly forwards. with your head resting lightly on the top so that you can turn it easily from one side to the other.

If you do have to sit at a desk for long periods beware of letting yourself slump over it.

Figure 6: Sitting Positions

FROM SITTING TO STANDING

- In order to rise to a standing position you will find it necessary to lean your body forwards. In doing so, try to keep your head in the same relationship to your spine as when it is upright. As the lean forward propels you to stand up, let the top of your head lead the way. *Do not* let your chin come up or let the small of your back hollow (see figure 7 on page 64).

The back of your neck should always be as long as
possible. Avoid pulling the back of your skull down into
a collapsed neck. This causes serious constriction and

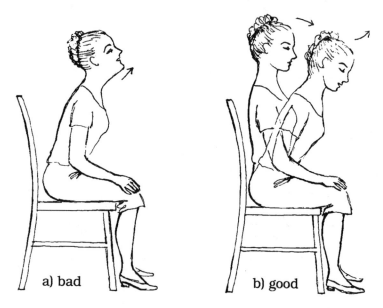

a) bad   b) good

Figure 7: Sitting to Standing

distorts the muscles of the throat, making the voice
sound old and stringy. When we are young a collapsed
neck soon gets counteracted by plenty of lively activity
- sports or dancing - but as we get older, the collapse
does not straighten out so readily and can easily become
permanent. A good prevention is to imagine you have an

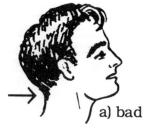
a) bad

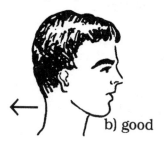
b) good

Figure 8: The Long Neck

eye in the back of your neck which needs to see over the top of your collar. As you turn your head, the 'eye' can survey the view behind you. Having stood up, remember to reverse the process when you sit down.

- Before sitting, make sure you can feel the front of the chair with the back of your legs. As you lower yourself onto the chair, let your whole spine *and* your head lean forward.

- Do not push your butt out in an ungainly fashion to 'find' the seat.

- When you are seated let your spine become upright, bringing your head with it. Then you can shift back on the seat if you need to.

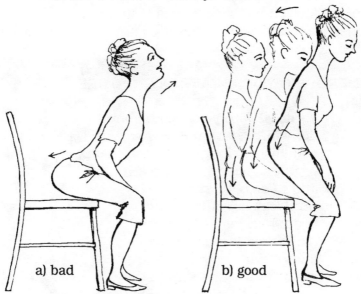

a) bad   b) good

Figure 9: Standing to Sitting

You will be surprised how many people sit down in the manner of Figure 9a. Look around and see what I mean. Then ask yourself if you do the same or not?

We sit and stand a great many times each day, during
which a lot of bad habits can accumulate unnoticed;
that is why I think it is important to give these movements more than a passing thought. Practise sitting and
standing as specified above until your mind is pro-
grammed to it, then incorporate the new ways as much
as possible into your everyday routine. The standing
movement should be light and buoyant, without strain;
the sitting movement should also be light and buoyant
so that you don't crash down onto the seat. (On the
London Underground I often bounce into the air when
someone sits down with a thud next to me!)

Once you have experienced the sheer pleasure of feeling
the upward flow from the bottom of your spine right up
into your neck, you are unlikely to let yourself slump
again. Apart from this, all sorts of shoulder tensions and
back problems will be alleviated and your voice will be
free from constriction.

IMPROVING YOUR STANDING POSTURE

1. Stand with your feet a shoulder width apart and your weight
equally distributed between them.
2. Take an easy deep breath
and raise both arms loosely
until they are above your
head. Feel your chest rise
naturally, lifting your ribs
away from your waist and
making as much space as
possible between your ribs
and your hips. Now stretch
your arms until they are
straight, right to the fingertips.
Keep breathing naturally;

Figure 10: Stand and Stretch

don't pull your abdomen in or push your butt out.
Even try standing on your toes to get that extra
gratifying stretch from fingers to toes.
3. Heels on the floor again, relax your fingers,
then your hands, followed by your wrists and
elbows until your upper arms are level with your
shoulders.

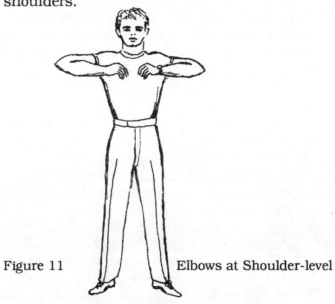

Figure 11   Elbows at Shoulder-level

4. Keeping your elbows at
shoulder level, ease
them back as far as they
will comfortably
go. Feel your
chest open
out and
consciou-
sly breathe
in it. Don't
let your
neck jut   Figure 12:
forward.

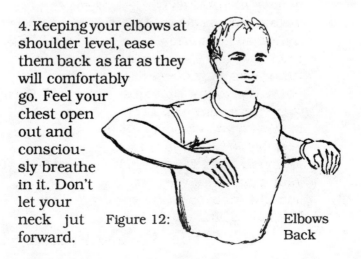

Elbows
Back

5. Still keeping your elbows level with your shoulders, bring them slowly forwards until they almost meet in front of you. As you do so, let the top of your spine curl forward and your head drop down a little. Feel your back open out and consciously breathe into it.

Figure 13: Elbows Forward

6. Uncurl your spine to its upright position, bringing your head with it. Let your arms fall loosely to your sides, leaving your chest buoyant.

Do this every day - it makes you feel really good!

Loosening

LOOSENING YOUR NECK, JAW AND SHOULDERS

- Remaining in the final position of the standing posture exercise, drop your head forward so that your chin is almost touching the top of your chest near your throat. This means releasing the tension in your neck muscles surrounding the top few vertebrae; otherwise you are standing upright.

- Slowly revolve your head to the left so that your left ear almost brushes your left shoulder. Take your head on round the back, letting your jaw fall open. Bring your head on round so that your right ear almost brushes your right shoulder and you end up in the starting position (looking at the floor).

You may experience a few creaks and crunches but this will do no harm provided your neck is relaxed and there is no forcing.

- Repeat the left-hand revolve followed by two right hand revolves. Always move your head slowly and remember not to keep your mouth closed, especially when your head is back. Finish in the starting position .

- With the back muscles of your neck, slowly

bring your head up to level so that you are looking
straight ahead of you. Pause.

• Leaving your jaw loose and passive, gradually
relax those neck muscles so that your head
slowly falls back over your collar (if you're wearing one).

• Don't let your jaw follow your head but feel
it separate from it just in front of your ears. You
should now be looking at a point about equivalent
to where the wall in front of you meets the ceiling with your jaw dropped open.

• Don't be tempted to raise your eyebrows; leave
your face uninvolved.

• Using the back muscles of your neck, bring
your head slowly up to the level position, feel it
coming towards your jaw — don't let your jaw
come to it! Pause.

• Relax your head slowly forward again. Repeat
this rocking backwards and forwards several
times, bearing in mind that when your head is
dropped forward your mouth is virtually closed,
and when it is dropped back your mouth is open
in a natural gape.

ROLLING DOWN YOUR SPINE

• Rock your head forwards and backwards twice,
feeling the weight of your head each time it drops.
Drop it forward a third time and let the weight of
your head pull your spine down like a drooping
plant. As you curl down the spine, let your
shoulders relax and your arms hang loose. Keep
your balance by letting your knees bend a little.

Figure 14:
The "Drooping
Plant"

• As you hang down from your waist gently shake
your head, shoulders and arms. Pause long
enough to feel how heavy your head is, hanging
like a coconut or weighty fruit on a stem, then
slowly uncurl your spine, letting your shoulders
and arms fall into place, your neck and head
coming up last.

Do this whole procedure several times at first and then
at least once a day. The ability to let your head hang
loose or float it lightly on the top of your spinal column
greatly increases its resonating capacity.

When you have rolled down your spine, as above, and
your head is hanging loose, it is a good idea, if you can
find a suitable partner, to get them to move your head
round for you. The best way is for them to cup your
forehead in the palm of their hand and gently lift it and
drop it an inch or two. You must try not to anticipate

what your partner is going to do. Don't make helpful movements, your head should be a dead weight. If you reverse roles with your partner and manipulate their head you will see what I mean and you will feel just how heavy the head is. And this is what you carry about all day. It's a wonderful feeling when you can let go.

LOOSENING YOUR THROAT MUSCLES

This exercise I call the 'GUG-GUGs', though it is more appropriate to think of it as a string of 'GA's' performed on an *intake* of breath. It follows on very well from the previous head-rolling and spine-rolling.

> 1. Standing comfortably, as before, let your head fall back and away from your jaw in a natural gape.

> 2. Prepare to breathe in through your mouth; before you do so, raise the back of your tongue against your soft palate, blocking the way. As you feel your diaphragm pulling down, release your tongue to its relaxed position so that your throat opens and the air goes in like a gasp.

> 3. Repeat one tongue-block and release per one breath until you've got the feeling and can do it easily.

> 4. Increase the number of block and releases to three like saying 'GA-GA-GA' on an *inward* breath — making sure your tongue flops back to zero between each one.

> 5. Utilize the breath you have taken and breathe out on three *whispered* 'K' sounds. The movement is similar except that 'G's' go backwards and 'K's' go forwards.

6. Now, with an easier tongue movement, do about seven whispered 'GA's' on a long breath *in*, and the same number of whispered 'K's' on the breath *out*.

This will loosen all the muscles round the larynx.

Do not breathe in first and then try to do the tongue movements.

About Breathing

It may seem odd that breathing should require so much of our attention, considering that we breathe throughout our lives from the first breath in, at birth, to the last breath out, at death. However, because most people tend to take their breathing for granted, they frequently allow it to get into bad shape - and a few deep breaths at the window in the morning is not the answer.

The Respiratory System, as we have seen, is a remarkable mechanism. It is perhaps at its most efficient when left to itself and the prime example of that is when we are asleep. Watching somebody sleeping — and I mean a normally healthy person and one who doesn't snore! — you will note that their breathing is almost imperceptible; the throat is relaxed and the chest hardly moves. Evidence of breathing is situated much more in the abdominal area — a gentle in and out.

Occasionally, the sleeper requires more oxygen, initiating a long, slow intake of breath, usually through the mouth and sometimes accompanying a change of position. The long expulsion of air that follows is in the manner of a sigh, sometimes even half vocalised if the vocal cords are partially closed. The sigh expulsion is important to consider; many singers are taught to vocalise on a sigh and it is just as salutory for speech.

It is generally agreed that breath goes in and comes out but there are a surprising number of ways of achieving this simple process — from sniffs to gasps and from sneezes to coughs.

Sitting at a desk, writing or typing, is not physically very demanding. Most likely, your mouth will be closed and the breathing will take place quietly through your nose. It is something that does not have to be thought about. If, however, some tricky problem arises, you will probably hold your breath for a moment and then suddenly let it out through your mouth.

Or the opposite may occur where you hold your breath while you consider the problem until you are forced (by your brain) to take a long, deep breath through your mouth, which amounts to a sigh. One stage further to this is the yawn, an intake of breath which is much more noticeable and very difficult to resist.

FREEING THE BREATH - LYING ON THE FLOOR

Before harnessing the breath into any form of vocalisation it is necessary to free the breathing rhythm of any gripping or holding and the best way to do that is consciously to breathe out — a long emptying exhalation. Feeling fairly empty in the middle, wait a moment until you feel the need to breathe in. This way, the breathing mechanism is set in motion without your making conscious interference. However, before we take this any further, let us put the whole body in an ideal state of relaxation by lying face upwards on the floor. If you don't like lying on the floor (or can't) you can do it on your bed but a hard surface is better.

> - With a couple of paperback books as a head-rest, lie flat on the floor. The paperbacks allow for

the natural curve at the top of the spine and prevent a cramping of the neck. As everyone's spine is different, you must judge for yourself, in the absence of an adviser, whether you need two books (usual), one book, or even three. In any case, the neck and throat should feel easy and unimpeded for the flow, back and forth, of the breath.

Figure 15: Lying Flat

As all healthy spines are slightly curved, it is, of course, not feasible to lie "flat" on the floor; if the legs are thrown out straight, the small of the back will inevitably rise a little off the floor - enough, in fact, to slide your flattened hand under. Do not try to adjust this but, should this area of the back get tired or feel uncomfortable, bring your feet nearer to your body by bending your knees until the soles of your feet are on the floor.

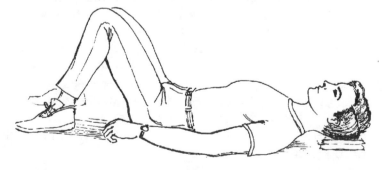

Figure 16: Knees Up

Choose whichever position you prefer. However, I think it is easier to achieve the following process of relaxation with the legs flat out.

1. Concentrate on your toes and let go of any tension in them. Take time over this and each succeeding point.

2. Relax your feet; then your ankles; then up your legs to your knees; then up your thighs to your hip joints. (Pay particular attention to your hip joints as they are notorious repositories of tension. Let them go with an outward release.)

3. Relax your lower abdomen - all round your waist - your diaphragm, and your ribs. (Let your ribs be entirely passive to the movement of your breath. There should be almost *no* movement in the upper chest.)

4. Transfer your attention to your fingers and release them of any tension.

5. Relax your hands; then your wrists; then up your arms to your elbows; then up to your shoulders. (Pay extra attention to your shoulders as they also harbour a great deal of tension. Take time to let them go.)

6. Relax your neck and your throat.

7. Relax your jaw and your tongue.

8. Relax your lips.

9. Relax your cheeks and your face.

10. Relax your eyes (open or closed, not active)

11. Relax your eye-brows and your forehead (let all the creases fall out) - and even relax your scalp.

12. Let all your tension drop away into the floor.

13. Finally, try to relax *inside* your head by letting go of your brain - always difficult to do at first.

14. Resist all busy thoughts and be content to <u>do</u> *nothing* for a moment. In this way you can achieve a splendid renewal.

SLEEP BREATHING

▪ After a few moments of lying in this pleasant limbo you should feel quite weightless, almost detached. However, allow your consciousness to be aware of your breathing. Take note of its gentle, even rhythm. As in sleep, the breaths will be small but deep,causing a gentle rise and fall in the area below the ribs — the solar plexus.

▪ Experience this sleep-breathing rhythm for a few moments and then, as in sleep when the brain requires more oxygen, take a deep sigh, letting your mouth open as you do so. Let your abdomen rise and your ribs expand from the bottom up. Release the breath slowly through your mouth and revert to the sleep-breathing rhythm. Repeat this a few times.

▪ Continue the sleep-breathing rhythm, inhaling through your mouth and nose and exhaling through your mouth on a small 'F' sound. This means bringing your bottom lip up and slightly in front of your upper front teeth. Do not in any way alter the rhythm, such as elongating the 'F' sound. No pushing or labouring; just let it happen. The 'F' serves to focus the breath column towards the front of your mouth and helps you to monitor it.

FROM SLEEP BREATHING TO PANTING

- From the sleep-breathing rhythm, very gradually begin to increase the speed, the breaths becoming smaller and lighter as you do so. Each breath,however small, should reach down to your diaphragm and solar plexus, in other words, your 'centre'. Here your muscles should be completely free to respond to the quickening movement of the breathing. In order to feel this, place one hand lightly on your abdomen, just below your ribs. Each breath, however quick and light, should cause your hand to rise and fall.
- If your muscles sieze up as you increase the speed, stop and begin again at a slower pace. Letting go of these abdominal muscles is particularly difficult for those people who do a lot of physical exercise such as weight-lifting or dancing. If you find this happens to you, be patient! As I said, the faster the breaths, the smaller and lighter they should become.
- Watch the movement of your abdominal muscles expanding when breathing in and contracting when breathing out.
- Continue getting faster and smaller and lighter until you are panting in a rapid, minute oscillation.
- Throughout all this the ribs should remain almost motionless.
- If you continually find the panting difficult to achieve, picture the way a dog pants and imitate it. You can even put your tongue out if it helps.

The 'Whispered HA'

The 'Whispered HA' is one of the most effective and useful of all the exercises for freeing the voice. Not only does it focus the released breath but it makes special demands of the jaw.

T-1

1. Make sure your jaw is dropped to repose level and ease it forward until your lower incisors are directly below your upper incisors (most people will need to move the jaw forward but there are exceptions).

2. Slowly bring the lower incisors up to touch the upper incisors — gently, no clenching.

3. Over this teeth-touching position, adopt a high, radiant smile — the corners of your mouth up and your eyes sparkling.

4. Keep the smile and very slowly lower your jaw, keeping it well forward. Feel your jaw descending vertically like a lift rather than dropping back towards your neck. As your jaw descends, slowly breath in to your waist.

5. When your jaw has descended as far as it will go (all your teeth should be showing) and your breath is fully taken, release the breath on a vigorous whispered 'HA'. *Do not close your mouth as you do so.*

The whispered 'HA' should sound free and spacious, the breath energy having come from the diaphragm — not the throat. After the 'HA' let the smile and your jaw revert to repose level or 'zero', as I frequently call it, before you start again.

6. Repeat, following the instructions 1 to 4 meticulously. These should be measured and slow; only 5 should be quick.

Later, you can do these 'Whispered HA's' with a quicker preparation and less smile. When necessary they can be done almost imperceptibly. For bringing the breath "up front" in readiness for clear speech, I cannot over-estimate their worth.

Phonation: From Breath to Voice

Phonation is the transformation of unvibrated breath into vibrated breath, producing vocal sound or Voice. It produces the basic vocal sound before the demands of speech are applied to it. In truth, unless phonation is achieved efficiently, with the tension neither too tight nor too slack, it is a waste of time practising articulation or trying to improve resonance, let alone working on actual speech, because phonation comes first. Yet it is something to which most of us give little or no thought. In fact, we take it for granted. We know that the idea of speaking to someone has only to flick into our mind and a voice will just materialize. However, think what a nasty shock you would get if one day you opened your mouth to speak and nothing happened. This would certainly be the case if you suddenly found yourself without a larynx.

The larynx, as we know, provides the 'stop' to the breath column (like the pea in a tin whistle), causing it to vibrate. It is a miraculous process which deserves our respect and some consideration if we are to achieve efficient rather than haphazard phonation.

SHAKING OUT BASIC VOCAL SOUND

1. Stand as before in an easy, upright position with your feet about a shoulder-width apart and your weight evenly distributed.

2. Place the tip of your tongue out on your lower lip,take a breath and vocalise a long, easy sound and let your head flop about loosely.

3. Take another breath and release another long sound (don't worry what vowel it is) and lift and flop your shoulders. Renew the breath and sound when necessary.

4. Keep the sound going and let the movement from your head and shoulders spread into your body and legs. Bend your knees and shake your pelvis. Don't worry that you may look and sound like a zombie. This exercise is for getting rid of tension and releasing the voice in its primitive state.

5. Renew the sound again, letting your tongue slide back into your mouth. Keep a gentle movement throughout your body and move the pitch up and down in an easy range and feel the vibrations filling your nasal cavities and skull, especially when you drop your head forward.

6. Renew the sound again and flop down your spine with your arms hanging loose until you are nearly bent double, your knees slightly bent as in the loosening exercise (P. 70).

7. Renew the sound again and unroll your spine, flopping your head and shoulders gently until you are upright.

DRUMMING AND PUMMELLING

This is another way of shaking the sound out of your
body and takes the form of gentle breast-beating. It can
be done standing or sitting.

  1. Take a deep easy breath and release it on a long
  sustained sound in the middle of your voice. With
  your fists loosely clenched, lightly tap the top of
  your rib-cage just below the collar bones. Keep
  tapping as long as the sound lasts.

  2. Renew the sound and extend the tapping down
  the centre of your rib-cage where the breast-bone
  is. Men can safely pummel all over their chests
  like Tarzan, but Jane should be more selective
  where she hits! Aim for the bony parts to wake up
  the resonance. This is wonderfully loosening and
  pleasing. Equally so is to apply the same treatment to your back, but a sympathetic partner is
  needed for this. While you vocalise, get someone
  to pummel (gently) all round the top of your back
  and shoulders. Pummelling the lower back should
  be confined to the centre, avoiding the kidney
  areas.

In the absence of a partner you can gently bounce your
back against a wall or door-post while you're vocalising
but don't do yourself an injury!

  3. On different days, repeat the above Tarzan
  exercise with different vowels such as EE, AY,
  AH, OH and OO.

  4. Continue making long, sustained sounds and
  gently prod your diaphragm with your fingers to
  create a rhythmic pulse.

5. Renew the sound and extend the prodding down to the abdomen, lowering your pitch as you go.

6. Renew the sound and with your thumb and fingers *gently* move your larynx from side to side to ensure that it doesn't stiffen up.

A Note on Phonetics
and the 'ER' Sound

'ER' is one of the most useful sounds for practising vocal freedom because it is a neutral, central vowel and is emitted when the tongue is at its most relaxed or when it is undecided. Indeed, it is during moments of indecision that this sound most frequently escapes our lips - amazingly frequently, in fact. We hear people doing it all the time when they pause to answer a question or think what to say.

How many times have we seen in printed dialogue in books and plays that little intrusive 'Er' to indicate hesitancy or indecisiveness. It is like the voice tuning up while the mind thinks what to say. Once the decision is made, the tongue knows where to go. However, the spelling of 'ER' as a voice exercise presents a problem because nearly everyone except the English will quite naturally pronounce the 'r', making it into a double sound.

In Anglo-Saxon pronunciation, the use of 'r' after a vowel was either meant to prolong the vowel or to temper it in some way. The 'r' was not itself pronounced as it would be in the Latin languages. Actually pronouncing the 'r', attractive as it may sound in, say, American or Scottish English, can reduce the clarity of the vowel because of the bunching up of the tongue in a retroflex action. For instance, take the word 'blurred' which authentically conveys its meaning in sound if the 'r's' are not pronounced. With them, the word is no longer so evocative of its meaning.

How then to spell the vowel-sound that exists in such words as 'earth', 'world', 'bird', 'cur' and 'her'. Each vowel is spelt differently but sounds more or less the same with the ever-present 'r' acting as a modifier. Take the 'r's' away and you would have very different words. In order to negate the pronunciation of 'r' in the 'ER' and 'HER' exercises, I have chosen not to use the phonetic symbol /3/, which could confuse people, but simply to cross the letter out; e.g. R̶ or r̶.

The International Phonetics Association, partly to solve this problem of multi-national pronunciation and spelling, devised a remarkable alphabet to represent just about every sound that can be uttered by the human voice from Florentine vowels to Hottentot clicks. This lengthy set of symbols is quite daunting and complicated to learn. Not only are all vowels and consonants and other vocal noises represented but their placement in the mouth or nose can be indicated. This is extremely useful for getting the authentic sound of a new language you may be learning but, fascinating as they are, this book is not about phonetics.

Efficient Phonation

Now that we have sorted out the sound of 'ER, you will find I use it as the starting-off point for many exercises and explorations of the voice. It is ideal because, as I have said, the tongue is in its most relaxed state, whereas 'EE' and 'AH' require more defined lingual positions which calls for a certain, if small, amount of effort.

This exercise follows on appropriately from the breathing exercises where you were lying on the floor. Having achieved complete freedom in your diaphragm and abdominal muscles with the panting, you can now harness the freed breath into vocal sound and monitor the result. Also, by building up the sound from mere breath, you can experience how to get the maximum effect with the minimum effort.

HARNESSING YOUR BREATH

T·2

1. Lie on the floor and let your breath revert to the easy sleep-breathing rhythm (on average, this rhythm is slightly faster than two seconds inhalation and two seconds exhalation).

2. Without altering the rhythm, breathe out on small, gentle 'F' sounds (no voice) with your lower lip slightly in front of your upper incisors. Do not force your breath out or slow it down. The 'F' is purely to monitor the exhalation.

3. At a given moment, when you feel like it, change the 'F' to a quietly whispered 'HER'. Continue on each successive breath.

4. When you feel like it, change the whispered 'HER' to a very quietly voiced 'HER'. Don't worry if it sounds a bit rough.

5. Compare the feeling of the whispered and the voiced 'HER' by alternating them. Any hoarseness or roughness should soon disappear. Do not be tempted to 'clear' your throat.

6. When you feel that the voiced 'HER' is clear, continue quietly on your voice without the whisper. Maintain the sleep-breathing rhythm which will keep each 'HER' relatively short.You should feel the sound vibrating above the middle of your tongue and infusing the facial sinuses.
(If at any time your mouth gets dry just pause, close your mouth and let the saliva return.)

7. Gradually make each 'HER' a little louder. Do not force, but feel more energy in the breath and more vibration in the front of your face. As you get louder, let the sounds be a little longer and the intake of breath equally so.

8. When you have got as loud as is comfortable on 'HER', change to a bright 'HAY'. Feel bright-eyed and cheerful, your face smiling. Increase the volume and the length of each 'HAY' gradually until they sound as loud as calling a friend across the street — "HAY!"

9. Increase the volume and length of each 'HAY' still more but avoid any feeling of pushing; let the stimulus of wanting to be heard provide the

necessary energy. Call the imaginary friend as though he is getting further and further away but keep as relaxed as possible and resist getting frantic. Each call should be a RELEASE rather than an effort. Breathe in as much air as you let out and make sure it hits the bottom of your lungs each time.

10. Continue calling out 'HAY' — each one louder and longer than the last — until they sound like prolonged cheers, emitted with freedom and pleasure.

CONSCIOUS ABDOMINAL EFFORT

T-3

▪ Still lying on the floor, breathe in and quietly voice at an easy, medium to low pitch a short, sharp 'HAY', consciously pulling in sharply your abdominal muscles and diaphragm to do so. Relax the muscles immediately afterwards.

▪ Repeat short, sharp 'HAY's' in groups of three — a fresh breath for each sound. Releasing the abdominal muscles after each 'HAY' will promote the replacement of the breath.

    HAY HAY HAY - pause
    HAY HAY HAY - pause etc.

▪ Repeat as above in groups of three but quite a bit louder, necessitating a stronger pull in of the abdominal muscles. Remember to release between each sound.

▪ Still keeping them short and sharp, repeat the 'HAY's' in groups of three very loudly, relying on the strong muscular pull-ins to supply the force. If you feel strain in your throat it means the abdominal muscles are not being used sufficiently.

As the 'HAY's' get louder the pitch will tend to rise. No harm in that so long as each 'HAY' carries with it a sense of *release*, as opposed to tightening up and squeezing the higher sounds out. (TAPE example of how it should *not* sound.) However, it is very productive to experiment with the loud 'HAY's' at low pitches. This is difficult at first, seeming well nigh impossible to those with naturally high voices but, provided the abdominal muscles do the work and not the throat, miraculous forces come together to make sounds you probably never thought you had! This is a highly effective way of achieving strong, authoritative tones.

NOTE: After lying on the floor for any length of time, always rise very slowly to prevent the blood rushing from your head and making you feel giddy. The best way is to roll onto your side, draw your knees up towards your chest, then sit up, then kneel, and then stand up - and enjoy doing it.

Finding Your Own Correct Pitch

A surprising number of people are unaware that they are not speaking at the correct pitch of their voices. They will go through life labouring unnecessarily, talking at a pitch that is not centred to their capacity, physique and personality. Not only will they be unaware of this displacement but most of the people hearing them will be unaware of it, too. It is the equivalent of someone hearing a piano for the first time and not realising that it would sound so much better if it were tuned. A truly centred voice, like a tuned piano, has a direct appeal to the listener. People with out-of-tune, off-centre voices are unlikely to exert that appeal and they will almost certainly hate hearing themselves on tape. They cannot believe it is them. "It can't be me," they say. Or, "I can't stand hearing my own voice." The voice they hear is completely different from what they expected.

A voice is a very personal possession — no two are identical, any more than two faces are. Voices can be grouped into types, the most obvious being that women have high voices and men have low ones. But some women have naturally low voices and some men have naturally high ones. Languages of various countries as well as regional accents will divide voices into groups but within these groups are personal characteristics which make one voice distinguishable from another.

The range of the speaking voice is considerably less than that of the singing voice yet, even in speech, it is surprising how low and how high a voice can go. It is not a question of pushing the voice up or down from its usual pitch, but of letting the vocal machinery work from top to bottom without hindrance.

Here is a way of exploring the extremities of your voice without losing touch with your 'centre'.

T-4

- Stand comfortably upright with your feet about a shoulder-width apart and your weight evenly balanced - the usual starting-off stance. Do a few head-rolls(as on P. 69) to loosen your neck and jaw. Leave your head dropped forward; with the back muscles of your neck, bring your head up to the level position, then let it fall gently back,leaving your jaw open and your tongue loosely flat (as in the Hard Palate section on P. 153).

Figure 17: Head Back (Long Neck)

The position of your head is as if you were trying to see the roof of your mouth in a mirror. In this way, your mouth lines itself up with your oro-pharynx and any vocal sound emitted can go straight into your mouth and hit the hard palate and alveolar ridge.

> • Breathe in slowly, lifting your soft palate as though you are yawning. Feel the breath go right down to your waist then release it on a low-pitched, fully-voiced 'HA'. Don't worry if the first one is a bit rough; this is usually due to disturbed mucus. Resist the temptation to cough but keep the back of your tongue low without pressing it down.

> • Keep your throat open and airy so that the sound isn't strangled and try the 'HA' again. If the sound seems muffled it may be because your head is too far back, in which case, bring it up a notch. The sound will also be muffled if it hits the soft palate, so be very conscious of aiming at the hard palate until you feel that the sound is clear.

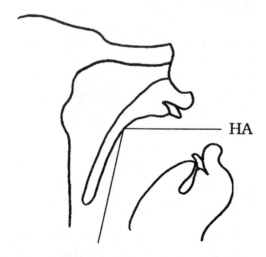

Figure 18: Head Back For HA

> • When you feel that the 'HA' is ringing clear, increase the number to three. Do them on one

breath and join them up like a formalised
laugh: HA-HA-HA

• Keep the pitch as low as possible, without
losing it 'down the drain'. Feel that you are
stroking the bottom of your voice: HA-HA-HA

• At this pitch the voice is commensurate with
resonance of the chest cavity (chest resonance)
and, if you place your hand on your breast bone
while you say 'HA-HA-HA', you should feel strong
vibrations there. Chest resonance is all the more
noticeable when the head is dropped back because this limits the head resonance.

• However, only low sounds of the so-called chest
register should be attempted with the head back.
A high sound would seriously stretch your throat
muscles, so don't try it — except perhaps once to
prove the point!

• For the middle of the voice, bring your head up
to level, your jaw lying passively under the descending upper teeth, leaving your mouth slightly
open. *Don't* bring your jaw up to meet your head.
Your tongue should be relaxed so as to produce
'ER' (see P. 86 — the vowel without the 'R').

• Take an easy, deep breath and, using a higher
pitch than for 'HA', release a nicely voiced 'HER'
right in the middle of your voice.

• Repeat it several times and feel it reach your
hard palate and infuse all your facial bones and
sinuses.

This is a very gentle sound and should be totally un-
forced. I call it the Face Voice, as opposed to the Chest

Voice or Head Voice, because it resonates from the middle of the face.

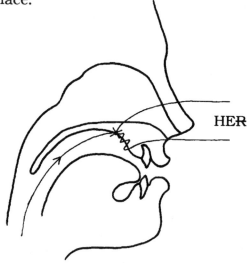

Figure 19: Head Level

▪ Take an easy, deep breath and say 'HER' three times on the one breath without separating them. HER-HER-HER.

▪ Repeat it several times, focusing the sound well forward into your mouth. Don't force it. It should not be loud.

▪ For the top of the voice, let your head fall forward. This will automatically narrow the gap between your teeth, and your tongue will be pushed forward so that it bends against the alveolar ridge in the position which produces the vowel 'EE'.

▪ With your head dropped forward, spread your lips in a slight smile. Take an easy, deep breath and, pitching rather higher in your voice than for 'HER',release a clear and ringing 'HEE'. Again, this should not be loud or in any way forced; the voice should feel as though it is passing through a resonant filter which is, in fact what it is doing.

- Repeat the 'HEE' several times and be aware of the intense vibrations between your tongue and the alveolar ridge.

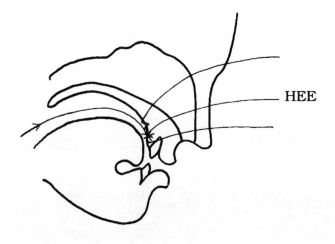

HEE

Figure 20: Head Forward

These vibrations should permeate the hard palate and infuse the whole of the nasal area, even reaching the top of the skull. You should be able to feel why the upper part of the voice is referred to as the Head Voice.

- Take an easy, deep breath and say 'HEE' three times on the one breath without separating them, as when laughing:
HEE-HEE-HEE

- Repeat several times, keeping the voice high and penetrating but without forcing it.

Compare your Head Voice with your Face Voice.

- With your head dropped forward, take a breath and say high in your voice: HEE-HEE-HEE

- With your head level, take a breath and say in the middle of your voice: HER-HER-HER.

- Repeat a couple of times, remembering to change the position of your head. Try to be aware of the difference in resonance of the two sounds as well as the pitch.

Compare your Face Voice with your Chest Voice.

- With your head level, take a breath and say in the middle of your voice: HER-HER-HER

- With your head back, take a breath and say low in your voice: HA-HA-HA

- Repeat a couple of times, remembering to change the position of your head. Again, try to be aware of the difference in resonance of the two sounds as well as the pitch.

Now that you have experienced the three main resonance qualities of the voice, put them together in sequence.

- With your head back, take a breath and say low in your voice: HA-HA-HA

- With your head level, take a breath and say in the middle of your voice: HER-HER-HER

- With your head forward, take a breath and say high in your voice: HEE-HEE-HEE

If we use two parallel, horizontal lines to represent the approximate top and bottom extremes of your voice and use dots to indicate the syllables, the exercise will read like this — [✔ indicates a breath]:

HA-HA-HA✔ HER-HER-HER✔ HEE-HEE-HEE
(Head back.....   level........   forward....)

▪ Now reverse it.

HEE-HEE-HEE HER-HER-HER HA-HA-HA
(Head forward.....   level........   back....)

Now try the three pitches in one breath, making a phrase of nine connected segments.

> ▪ Commence with your head back, bring it to level on the third 'HA' and drop it forward on the third 'HER'. Let the third syllable of each group slide up to the pitch of the next group:

HA-HA-HA-HER-HER-HER -HEE-HEE-HEE
(Head back..   level.......   forward....)

- Take a breath and reverse the sounds, remembering to bring your head up to level on the third 'HEE' and to drop it back on the third 'HER'.

Let the third syllable of each group slide down to the pitch of the next group:

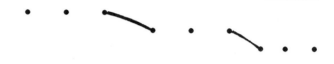

HEE-HEE-HEE-HER-HER-HER-HA-HA-HA

- Repeat several times, breathing in between each set of three positions.

- On one breath, run the three sounds together in a long slide or glissando, commencing with your head back and slowly bringing it up and finishing with it dropped forward. Only one 'H' is necessary at the beginning:

HA----- ER-----EE---

- Reverse it, commencing with your head forward and slowly bringing it up and finishing with it dropped back:

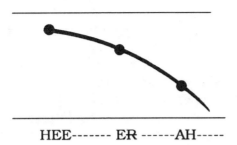

HEE------- ER ------AH-----

- Repeat these slides, alternating going up, then down, with a breath between each:

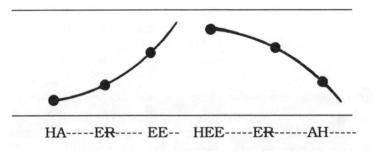

HA-----ER----- EE--   HEE-----ER------AH-----

By now, you should have slid through the whole range of your voice, from the bottom to the top and from the top to the bottom.

The remarkable fact about this exercise is that the positioning of the head is not only suitable to the pitching of the voice but that each position automatically causes the tongue to assume the required vowel position — provided you don't interfere with it.

This doesn't mean that in normal speech you will fling your head backwards or forwards every time you say an 'AH' or an 'EE' but, as an exercise, it is expedient in helping you *find* the correct pitch and vowel.

EXPLORING THE BOTTOM OF YOUR VOICE

As in a musical instrument, extreme tension produces a high pitched voice whereas a slackening of tension will lower it. In a good flexible voice there is no fixed floor or ceiling, as could be seen from the previous exercise. Voices differ from day to day; they can be affected by the weather, or worry, or nerves; they can be affected by happiness, or joy, or success.

The vocal cords dictate the pitch of the voice but if there is tension round them the voice will be pushed up or it will sound thin. It is easier for singers to be aware of this because they have definite notes to aspire to. They soon learn that low notes can only be attained by a loosening of tension and, though it is understandable to tense up for the high notes, they also learn that any tension other than in the diaphragm and the vocal cords will wreck those notes. The speaker doesn't have this discipline and frequently doesn't know where he is in the scale of things - if he even gives it a thought. We shall now give it considerable thought in order to explore the bottom of the voice by releasing tension.

> ■ Stand or sit in a good, upright but comfortable position. From the pace of your natural breathing, consciously breathe in through your mouth and nose and release the breath through your mouth in a voiceless sigh. Repeat this several times.

> Next, take a slightly longer breath and release on a gently voiced 'HER'. Don't force this sound, but repeat it until it is clear by releasing it away from the back of your throat and letting it permeate the nasal cavities.

> ■ If it seems to rattle in your throat, whisper

the 'HER' several times before you voice it again. It sometimes helps to bring the sound forward by slightly funnelling the cheeks and mouth in the French manner.

▪ Using the same sound 'HER', say it quietly in the middle of your voice and then let it slide downwards:

HER ------------

▪ Repeat this a few times then, gauging where you stopped at the bottom, say the 'HER' there and let it slide upwards:

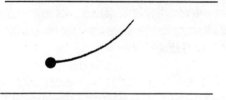

HER ----------

▪ Alternate the two slides several times, taking a breath between each.

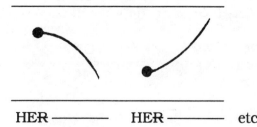

HER ———   HER ———   etc.

- Now do a sequence of downward slides
from the middle of your voice, getting
lower each time — a breath between each :

HER—   HER—   HER—   HER—   HER—

- Try to feel as though you are unwinding and
loosening, flopping your head and shoulders a
little. You should be so relaxed that you feel
drowsy. However, don't let your voice drop so low
that it becomes croaky; keep it clear. Aim to find
the lowest level of your voice before it loses quality
or disappears. It should be like the bottom string
of a guitar — open and free.

- When you have found the 'bottom string' of
your voice, feel that you are stroking it to make it
sound. Repeat the 'HER' slowly and quietly, as
low as you can, a breath for each one.

- Continue stroking the low 'HER' sounds as
above, without any visible effort or facial movements then, taking care not to raise the pitch or
increase the energy in any way, try other short
words in the same manner. If you tense up trying
to think what words to say, try counting 1 to 10,
with a breath between each:

HER ´ HER ´ HER ´ ONE ´ TWO ´
THREE ´ FOUR ´ FIVE ´ SIX ´ SEVEN ´
EIGHT ´ NINE ´ TEN ´

- Now extend the vocabulary adding other words.

Keep them short and avoid getting animated;
keep relaxed and drowsy. If random words
don't come easily to your mind, let your eyes
wander round the room or wherever you happen
to be and, whatever they catch sight of, say
it. Although the voice is low key, both in pitch and
effort, don't slur the words; keep them short and
clear. Here is an example of the progression
through from the low, relaxed 'HER'.

HER ✓ HER ✓ HER ✓ ONE ✓ TWO ✓ THREE ✓
FOUR ✓ FIVE ✓ SIX ✓ SEVEN ✓ EIGHT ✓ NINE ✓
TEN ✓ CHAIR ✓ TABLE ✓ DESK ✓ LAMP ✓
FLOOR ✓ MAT ✓ WALL ✓ WINDOW ✓ etc.

When you are comfortable using your voice at this low
premium, practice this exercise walking along the street,
or wherever, and read longer words off placards and advertisements — whatever you see. It is most beneficial in
removing the kind of tension in a voice that keeps it
unnecessarily high.

✳

Resonance:
The Benefit of Humming

Most people know what it is to hum a tune without ever giving it a thought; it is a way of singing without having one's mouth open, making it almost private. Many of us will hum quite absent-mindedly as we involve ourselves in some task when we wouldn't dare open our mouths and actually sing. People hum for different reasons of which three, I would venture to say, are paramount: they are either happy or they are concentrating or they are nervous. Emotionally speaking, humming is a release of tension; it is a pleasant sensation; it oils the feelings. What perhaps is not generally realized is that it is one of the most effective ways of improving the resonance of the voice. With the lips closed, the initial vibration of the vocal cords (the fundamental) can resound and rebound through all the cavities of the skull and thus increase in amplitude. Even done casually with little or no thought, humming will enhance the fundamental; with a little forethought and preparation it can be sensational!

We all know that in order to hum, the lips should be sealed — what the French call bouche fermée — however, the bouche should not be so fermée as to be clamped shut. While the lips are sealed the lower jaw should be loosely dropped as far as comfort will allow, thus making a large vibrating chamber of the mouth. Humming may seem to be predominantly concerned with the nose but without the involvement of the mouth a great deal of sound is lost. It is therefore important that, when humming, the back of the tongue doesn't rise and block the mouth off. There are ways of checking this which I shall come to in due course.

INITIATING THE HUMMING SOUND

T-6

- Take a breath and say in a good rounded voice the word 'HUM'.

- Now lightly seal your lips and, as you breathe in, lower your jaw to a comfortable extremity.

- Without unsealing the lips, again say the word 'HUM', letting the 'H' aspirate itself down your nose, followed by the humming sound.

- Repeat the process at different pitches, always making sure that you aspirate the 'H' down your nose.

If you put the back of your hand a few inches in front of your nose as you do this you should feel a sharp downdraft from the 'H' which will cease as soon as the breath vibrates into vocal sound.

- Lightly seal your lips, lowering your jaw as you breathe in; aspirate a low-pitched 'HUM' down your nose; increase the energy of the sound and let the pitch rise in a long curve and then drop down again.

- To increase the "buzz" in your sinuses, try to imitate the sound of a cow (or a bull) with long, low hums.

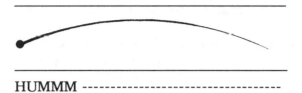

HUMMM ----------------------------------

Repeat several times, making the sound as cow-
like as possible. Think of the animal's long nose
and immense resonance area.

CHECKING YOUR TONGUE

It is a common fault, while humming, for the tongue to
rise and block off the mouth, thus robbing the sound of
half its volume.

The diagram shows how the vibrations from the unbloc-
ked mouth reach the facial sinuses through the hard
palate.

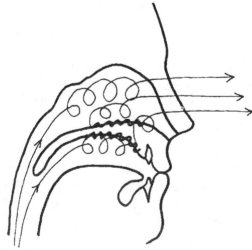

Figure 21: Humming Vibrations

Unfortunately, you cannot see your tongue while you are humming and it is not easy to feel with any degree of accuracy where it is. The obvious solution is to open your mouth and take a look in the mirror; if you are still humming when your mouth is open then your tongue is definitely blocking at the back. The nearest spelling for this sound is 'NG'.

- Do another long 'HUM' and, this time, if you are still making the 'NG' sound when your mouth is open, consciously separate your tongue from the roof of your mouth until you are making a good clear 'AH'.

- Alternate 'NG' and 'AH', first of all detached from each other: NG AH NG AH NG AH etc. Then joined up in a long sound: NG-AH-NG-AH-NG-AH-NG-AH etc. Register the sensation of your tongue touching your soft palate and separating from it. The two sounds should be markedly different.

- Check your tongue again in mid-hum. If it still persists in clinging to the roof of your mouth, take a good breath and say (or sing) a long 'AH'. During the 'AH', bring your lips together to produce a humming sound. Separate your lips again and close them several times on the one sound and try to get the feel of the position of your tongue.

- Reverse the procedure: lightly seal your lips, lowering your jaw as you breathe in. Aspirate a long 'HUM' down your nose — hum an actual note if you can. About half way through the sound, let your lips open several times. At each separation of your lips a clear vowel, preferably 'AH', should be heard: HMM-AH-MM-AH-MM-AH-MM-AH-MM-AH etc.

- When you have mastered this try some other
vowels: HMM-OO-MM-OO-MM-OO-MM-OO etc.
HMM-EE-MM-EE-MM-EE-MM-EE etc
HMM-AY-MM-AY-MM-AY-MM-AY etc.

THE 'MUH-NUH-MUH-NUH'S'   T-7

Both 'M' and 'N' make a humming sound in their
pronunciation and alternating them in slow or quick
succession is a good way of building up resonance in the
facial sinuses. The 'N' hum, of course, has the tongue
up, which we have been at pains to keep down; but note,
that for 'N', it is the front of the tongue that is up, not the
back, thus allowing some sound into the mouth under
the hard palate.

> - Alternate a succession of 'M' and 'N' hums fairly
> slowly (not quite as slowly as one per second),
> elongating the hum and minimizing any vowel
> sound to the flick between the two positions.
> Start quietly and build up the resonance on each
> succeeding change of position. Do not make your
> voice louder but let the resonance increase:

Resonance:

Articulation: MMM-NNN-MMM-NNN-MMM-NNN-MMM-
                                                etc.
The line of articulation is broken by the articulations
themselves but the resonance should be one continuous
sound.

> - Repeat now a little faster and be conscious of
> the continuous resonance over the articulations.

Resonance: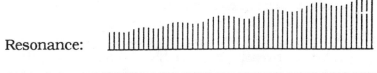

Articulation: MM-NN-MM-NN-MM-NN-MM-NN-MM-NN-
                                                    etc.
  • Try it now as fast and as long as you like

Resonance:

Articulation: M-N-M-N-M-N-M-N-M-N-M-N-M-N-M-N
                                                    etc.
Always feel the sound in your face and head *not*
your throat.

Another way to ensure that hummed sounds are as far
forward in the resonators as possible is to block them
momentarily before releasing them — as follows:

  ▪ Lightly seal your lips, lowering your jaw as you
  breathe in. When your inhalation is complete,
  seal your nose with thumb and forefinger, locking
  the breath inside. Now prepare to say the word
  'HUM'. Let the 'H' build up a small degree of
  compressed air in your nose and, as you begin to
  vocalise,release your nostrils so that the sound
  bursts forth of its own volition. Do not force the
  pressure and be sure to aim it right into your nose
  or you may 'pop' your ears which is most unpleasant. In other words, let the air pressure in your
  nose initiate the sound.

  ▪ When you have got the feeling of these 'nasal
  bursts', try them in different lengths and pitches,
  replacing the breath, through your nose, between each one. For instance, a string of short

bursts will require a short sniff of replacement between each sound.

With regard to pitch, you will notice that the higher tones demand more breath pressure but the mere thought of the pitch intended should ensure the pressure is right. Damage is done by adding more than is necessary. That is why it is best to keep loose and almost offhand doing these exercises.

- Try some long, nasal burst hums, starting high in the voice and sliding down to the bottom. Reverse the procedure by starting low in the voice and sliding high - as high as the voice wants to go and no higher. Make sure that you sustain the initial "buzz" right through to the end of each sound. Don't let the vibrancy recede or collapse.

- To help you sustain the resonance right through the sound, try a long nasal burst hum as above. This time, however, as soon as you have released the pinched nostrils, pinch them together briefly, several times during the hummed sound.

- Using the principle of the last exercise, perform a long hum. After the initial burst, briefly pinch your nostrils closed twice more and then leave open, making a phrase of two short sounds and a long one.

CAUTION: Do not force or overdo this exercise. If you do happen to 'pop' your ears, leave off for the time being and do something else.

- Return to the easy, relaxed 'HUMS'. Keep them fairly short, like sighs released down your nose.

• Try them in a casual manner when you are walking, or driving, or doing some pleasant task.

• In the same casual way, repeat the 'MUH-NUH-MUH-NUH's' quietly but intensely.

LOOSE LIPS AND FORWARD RESONANCE T-8

• Take a breath and blow out through loosely closed lips, making a sound like a horse: PRRRRR

• Do the same again only this time use your voice as well: PRRRRR

• Repeat this and add a 'HUM' to the end of it, letting the sound gather momentum: PRRRRRHUM

• Now add three 'M's' and a long MAH: PRRRRRHUM M M M MAH

• Repeat this several times and feel the build-up of tone into your resonators. Remember that the 'R's' are not really 'R's' but flapping lips. If in doubt, LISTEN TO THE TAPE.

• Say the phrase in your upper-middle register and repeat it many times (a breath for each), lowering it gradually each time until you reach the bottom string of your voice.

HUMMING DOWN AND UP YOUR SPINE

Humming down and up your spine is a pleasure to do and encourages the vocal vibrations into your head:

- Take a deep breath and hum a note - any comfortable note will do. Keep humming and drop your head forwards onto your chest and let the weight of your head pull your spine down like a drooping plant (see P. 70). Keep your shoulders relaxed and let your head hang loose like a coconut.

- Take another breath (don't lift your head to do so) and hum the same note again.If someone could gently pummel your upper back it would be ideal but, otherwise, gently shake yourself about to loosen up the sound.

- Take another breath and once again hum the same note. Keep humming as you slowly uncurl your spine, letting your shoulders and arms fall into place, your neck and head coming up last. As you bring your head up to level, let it lift away from your jaw so that your mouth opens and the humming becomes a vibrant 'AH'.

Repeat this at various pitches and you will feel really good.

NASAL RESONANCE: THE 'PINCHED EE'

A voice with little or no nasal resonance will sound inevitably flat due to the lack of upper partials or harmonics in the resonance chambers. The combinations of these harmonic frequencies are what distinguishes one musical instrument from another or one particular voice from another.

The 'pinched EE' is an exercise that is quite easy to do but difficult to describe in terms of sound so, when in doubt, listen to the tape. The principle is to concentrate the voice into the nasal cavity instead of the mouth.

☛ Sit down and, keeping your back long and straight, lean forward and support youself with one elbow on your knee — similar to Rodin's statue, The Thinker.

T-9

☛ With the hand of your supporting arm, pinch the nostrils of your nose together so that they are closed.

Figure 22: Pinching the Nose Closed

☛ Take a breath through your mouth down to your waist.

☛ Prepare your tongue to say 'EE' but raise it at the back as well, almost closing your mouth off from your throat in order to achieve the required intensity in your nasal cavity.

☛ Keeping your nose pinched, say three short 'EE's' on one breath into your nose.

☛ Do this again but with a high smile showing all your top teeth. This is to encourage vibrations into the sinuses.

It is not a pleasant sound — kids sound like it when they talk and hold their noses — but it is efficient. We are treating the naso-pharynx and nasal cavity like an organ pipe that is closed at one end; the sound pulse enters the narrow lip at the bottom of the tube which builds up a slight extra pressure. This compression travels the length of the tube until it hits the closed end which makes it reflect back until it finds its way out of the opening, visible at the front of all organ pipes.

In doing the 'pinched EE', the sound pulse initiated by the larynx travels up to the front of the nasal cavity and behind the sinuses before bouncing back to find an exit through the narrowed passage into the mouth where it is free to communicate with the outside air.

Continue as above, in the sitting position, leaning forward and pinching your nose. Take care there is no tension under your jaw and, if you feel the least strain in your throat, leave off for a while and do something else.

> ► Do a long 'pinched EE', starting low and sliding up to as high as is comfortable. Note how your abdomen pulls in as you get higher. (If it doesn't, you may strain your throat, so make sure it does.)
>
> ► Start the 'pinched EE' high and slide down to the bottom. This time your abdomen should be firm at the start and slacken as you descend.
>
> ► Repeat the slides up and down several times.
>
> ► Do several short 'pinched EE's' at various pitches.
>
> ► Do a long 'pinched EE' at a level pitch as though on a note.

☛ Do long 'pinched EE's' on definite, different notes. (PIANO NOTES ON TAPE)

All these 'pinched EE's' sound fairly unpleasant but, like nasty tasting medicine, they will do you a power of good.

THE TRANSITION FROM 'PINCHED EE' TO 'FREE EE'

☛ Start a 'pinched EE', as before, on a long note and, about halfway through, lower the back of your tongue so that the 'EE' readily flows into your mouth. (If you find this difficult, reverse the process: with your nose pinched, start with a long oralized 'EE' and then raise the back of your tongue so that the 'EE' is pushed into your nose.)

The contrast between the nasal and the oral 'EE' should be very marked. Do it several times and relish the transition.

NASALIZING AND ORALIZING   T-10

☛ Pinch your nose closed and say:
MEE-NEE-MEE-NEE-MEE-NEE-MEE-NEE
This will sound very nasal as it is but do it again and consciously nasalize it as much as possible:
MEE-NEE-MEE-NEE-MEE-NEE-MEE-NEE

☛ Repeat this but this time try to de-nasalize it by oralizing the 'EE's' and releasing them from the nasality of the 'M's' and the 'N's' which should be kept short.
MEE-NEE-MEE-NEE-MEE-NEE-MEE-NEE

(Pinching the nose makes this easy to monitor.)

☞ With your nose still closed, say the following
entirely nasalized:
MANY MEN CAME TO THE MEETING.

This is fairly easy because of so many 'M's' and 'N's'. It
is not so easy to oralize the same sentence but the
mental exercise is invaluable. Try it three different ways:

1. With the nose closed and entirely nasalized:
MANY MEN CAME TO THE MEETING.

2. With the nose closed and as oralized as possible:
MANY MEN CAME TO THE MEETING.

3. Let go of the nose and let it ring out, using
nasal and oral resonance:
MANY MEN CAME TO THE MEETING.

That should sound and feel good. Now take a sentence
that has no 'M's' or 'N's' in it and try it in three different
ways:

1. With the nose closed and without any nasality: HE IS A VERY GREAT ARTIST.

2. With the nose closed and entirely nasalized:
HE IS A VERY GREAT ARTIST.

3. With the nose open using nasal and oral
resonance:
HE IS A VERY GREAT ARTIST.

Here there will not have been a great deal of difference
in 1 and 3 except that 3 will have added resonance.
☞ Finally, pinch your nose closed and count from
one to ten in clear, ringing tones. This produces
a Positive Voice.

Only ONE, SEVEN, NINE and TEN should indicate that your nose is closed and they should be as oralized as possible. Use a breath for each numeral. Each one should be brisk and strong:

ONE TWO THREE FOUR FIVE SIX SEVEN EIGHT NINE TEN

By now you should fully understand the difference between nasal and oral resonance and to be able to maximize the use of both.

Vibrato: Sustaining the Tone

We know from physics that vocal sound is caused by thousands of tiny puffs of air forcing their way through the closed vocal cords and that the breath pulse is achieved by the release of stronger puffs of air at regular intervals along the vocal line. It is the regularity of these stronger puffs that makes a singing voice sound vibrant and secure. This is known as vibrato.

Now vibrato is a dirty word to many people who merely echo what they've heard said about bad singers: "What a terrible vibrato!" True, a vibrato can be terrible if it is uneven or faulty, but it can also be beautiful if it is even and free. After all, 'vibrato' is the Italian word for 'vibration' and a voice cannot exist without vibration. If this vibration sags or has sound-wave frequencies that are too widely spaced, the pitch will deteriorate into a wobble or a tremolo. It used to be a maxim among singers that "a vibrato is a virtue but a tremolo is a vice."

Every level of pitch has its own frequency of sound-wave which will happen quite naturally provided the voice or instrument is not interfered with or inhibited. These natural frequencies can, however, be further enhanced by a little 'outside' help. This is never more obvious than the string-player's hand on the strings of his instrument. You cannot fail to have noticed the oscillating wrist of say, a cellist, whose lower notes require a slower, wider movement.

A voice without vibrato is a dead voice; this is just as true of the speaking voice as it is of the singing voice.

DOTS AND PULSES

Bearing in mind the thousand of tiny puffs of air forcing their way through the closed vocal cords, I have always found it helpful to imagine the vibration of the voice as a string of closely placed dots travelling across a space. If the voice is vibrating well, whether speaking or singing, the string of dots will proceed horizontally until the end of the phrase:

If the voice is not vibrating well or the breath is uneven in its support, the string of dots may sag in places resulting in poor tone and faulty pitch:

Or it may even end up on the floor, so to speak:

Maintaining the dots at a horizontal level is entirely dependent on the support of breath energy which should be firm and evenly flowing. In turn, this breath energy is dependent on the diaphragm continually pressing against the abdominal muscles, causing a kind of nuclear fission.

By separating the voice into short, detached components, we are, in effect, pulling the dots apart which, when strung together, make up a longer sound. This isn't as easy as it may seem. For instance, it is quite a challenge to make a short vocal sound (as short as possible) and to repeat it a number of times at regular intervals at exactly the same length and at exactly the same pitch. In fact, it is impossible; inevitably there will be some variation, however hard you try. Nevertheless, the discipline of *trying* is immensely valuable as an exercise in control. Try saying 'OH' five times in exactly the same way and see how you get on. You might well say "Why is it necessary?" But the point is, *can* you do it? After a few attempts you soon begin to recognize any discrepancies. With a tape recorder it is surprising what differences you can spot both in pitch and quality.

If you can do a series of evenly spaced dots that are relatively identical, it stands to reason that putting the dots together again will produce a long sound with a pulse.

By imposing our own speed to this pulse we are applying the equivalent to the string-player's wrist which will induce vibrato where none exists or enhance what vibrato there is.

T-11

First of all we shall vocalize *one* dot in preparation for a string of five.

> • Say 'HUH!' quietly, as though you are being sceptical.

> • Repeat the 'HUH!' with your mouth closed so that the 'H' aspirates down your nose, as in the humming exercises. The sound should be very short but have a 'ping' in it.

> • Once you have got the feeling of the 'ping', do five in a row on one breath; keep your lips sealed and

your jaw slightly down. These 'vocalized H's' should be very short and evenly separated — a quick walking pace:

(lips sealed) HUH HUH HUH HUH HUH
            >   >   >   >   >
        (1   2   3   4   5)

(The sign ' > ' is a stress mark)

• Repeat. Try to make them all exactly alike in length and pitch — like a machine. If you have any doubts as to how these exercises sound, LISTEN TO THE TAPE.

• Repeat the five sounds but join them up into one long humming sound with five strong pulses or beats:

(lips sealed) HMM—MM—MM—MM—MM—
        >   >   >   >   >
      (1   2   3   4   5)

Choose any easy middle pitch and make sure there is no break in the sound - move along the line from beat to beat.

The result should be pleasing and easy to do.

As a firm foundation for the pulse, be sure to keep your diaphragm firmly pressed against your abdominal muscles until the sound is finished. Then you must relax.

• When you are comfortable with the hummed version, do the same on the following eight major vowels — with your mouth open, of course — first of all detached and then joined up.

1) ER   ER   ER   ER   ER
   >   >   >   >   >
   (1   2   3   4   5)
   ER---ER---ER--ER--ER---
   >   >   >   >   >

2) EE   EE   EE   EE   EE
   >   >   >   >   >
   EE-- EE--EE-- EE-- EE---
   >   >   >   >   >

('eh' 3) eh   eh   eh   eh   eh
as in   >   >   >   >   >
'bed')   eh--- eh----eh-- eh-- eh---
          >   >   >   >   >

('a'   4) a   a   a   a   a
as in   >   >   >   >   >
'cat')   a----a----a-----a---a---
          >   >   >   >   >

5) AH   AH   AH   AH   AH
   >   >   >   >   >
   AH--AH---AH--AH-- AH--
   >   >   >   >   >

6) AW   AW   AW   AW   AW
   >   >   >   >   >
   AW--AW---AW--AW---AW---
   >   >   >   >   >

7) OH   OH   OH   OH   OH
   >   >   >   >   >
   OH-- OH--OH-- OH---OH---
   >   >   >   >   >

8) OO   OO   OO   OO   OO
   >   >   >   >   >
   OO- -OO--OO---OO--OO----
   >   >   >   >   >

Now a much faster and louder vibrato. This will probably make your voice go higher because of the increased energy but try various pitches that are comfortable.

• Breathe in slowly till your diaphragm and abdominal muscles are firm and vibrate the 'HMM' sound as fast and as loud as you can and with considerable vehemence for nine pulses - or even more. The rhythm must be absolutely even, like a machine gun. This will depend entirely on the firmness of your diaphragm pressing against your abdominals throughout the sound. Then relax. Remember, it should be one long sound: (lips sealed)

HMM-MM-MM-MM-MM-MM-MM-MM-MM
  >   >   >   >   >   >   >   >   >
(1   2   3   4   5   6   7   8   9)

Check with TAPE that you are making the right sound, then repeat the process using the same eight major vowels as before:

1) ER—ER—ER—ER—ER—ER—ER—ER—ER
  >   >   >   >   >   >   >   >   >
(1   2   3   4   5   6   7   8   9)
2) EE EE EE EE EE EE EE EE EE
  >   >   >   >   >   >   >   >   >
3) eh---eh-- eh---eh--- eh---eh---eh---eh---eh
  > >   >   >   >   >   >   >   >
4) a----a----a---- a-----a-----a---a-----a---a
  > >   >   >   >   >   >   >   >
5) AH--AH--AH--AH---AH--AH--AH---AH--AH
  > >   >   >   >   >   >   >   >
6) AW--AW--AW-AW--AW--AW--AW--AW--AW
  > >   >   >   >   >   >   >   >
7) OH--OH--OH--OH--OH--OH--OH--OH--OH
  > >   >   >   >   >   >   >   >
8) OO--OO--OO--OO--OO--OO--OO--OO--OO
  > >   >   >   >   >   >   >   >

These are most exhilarating to do and will make your voice ring out!

✳

Vowels and Consonants

Vowels, consonants, segments, phonemes, syllables and allophones are all phonetic labels for the sound of different parts of words and, in the pursuit of a good voice and more effective speaking, I think it is time well spent to examine briefly these components that go together to make speech. Merely becoming familiar with them promotes a greater nicety in pronunciation.

There are two distinct ways of looking at vowels and consonants: one is how they look on paper and the other is how they sound.

Those of us who think we understand about vowels and consonants are often at a loss when it comes to describing them. The most simplistic view is that vowels are 'tone' and that consonants are 'noise'. Another view is that vowels are the musical parts of words — they can be sung — whereas most consonants are too short to be sung and others cannot be sung at all; they are brief sounds punctuating or accompanying vowels in order to form words.

A more official criterion of distinction between vowels and consonants is that of *stricture*, which means a temporary narrowing or closure of the speech tract causing audible friction which is characteristic of nearly all consonants.

Vowels, on the other hand, are pure unrestricted tone and, in a well produced voice, are devoid of friction.

VOWELS

In describing vowels, it is no good simply saying 'A,E,I,O,U' and leaving it at that. These are merely five letters of our alphabet which, with the aid of 'Y' and 'W', try to represent a minimum of twenty vowel sounds or phonemes. Indeed, it soon becomes apparent that the alphabet we use is totally inadequate for the number of sounds it has to represent.

Vowel sounds are nearly always made with voiced, egressive air - that is to say, air which is coming out of the lungs and up through the vocal cords and this travels unimpeded over the centre line of the tongue. The miracle of all this is how the vocal tone is transformed into one vowel or another, achieved mostly by the position of the tongue and the consequent modification in shape of the primary resonating chambers, namely the pharynx, the nasal cavity and the mouth. The lips, too, visibly change their shape for many of the vowels, particularly those that are rounded such as 'AW', 'OH' and 'OO'. These changes of shape produce specific sound intensities in particular frequency regions which provide the formants that distinguish the acoustic characteristics of one vowel from another. These formants also help us to distinguish one person's voice from another.

With the use of only five letters of the alphabet, it is always a problem to indicate on paper the exact pronunciation of the various vowels so that we have to rely on examples in word context to give us the clue, e.g. 'u' as in 'cup'.

Vowels can be spoken singly or in pairs or in threes. A single sound is known as a monophthong; a pair, meaning one sliding to another, is a diphthong; a slide of three sounds is a triphthong. If you say 'Ah', that is a monophthong; if you say 'Ow!', that is a diphthong consisting of 'AH+OO'; if you say 'Hour', that is a triphthong consisting of 'AH+OO+ER'.

T-12

Monophthongs — there are eleven of these with 'OH' making a possible twelfth. These words identify their sounds:

> 1.bead 2.bid 3.bed 4.bad 5.balm 6.pot 7.but
> 8.paw 9.boat 10.boot 11.put 12.pearl

The diagram below represents a side view of the mouth, squared up like a map, and the approximate place where each monophthong is formed by the position of the tongue:

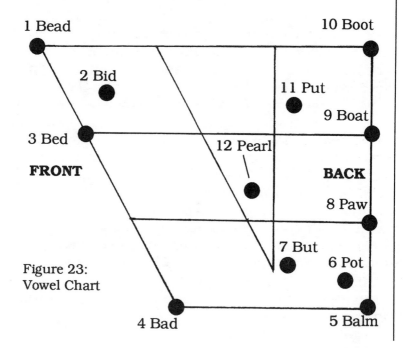

Figure 23:
Vowel Chart

Diphthongs — there are nine of these counting 'OH' which is usually pronounced as a diphthong and each one is a slide from one monophthong to another. The numbers refer to the chart (Figure 23):

say = 3+1 or 2	near = 1+7
so = 9+10	bear = 3+7
sigh = 5+1 or 2	pour = 8+7
cow = 5+10 or 11	poor = 10+7
boy = 8+1 or 2	

Triphthongs - there are not a great many of these and some of them are debatable. Here are four examples:

hour = 5+10+7 or 12	fire = 5+1+7 or 12
lower = 9+10+7 or 12	lawyer = 8+1+7 or 12

It is interesting to note that the commonest vowel sound in English is impossible to spell. It is what I call a neutral vowel and it occurs in many unstressed syllables such as the second syllable in 'alphabet' and the first and last syllables in 'banana' and 'performance'. Although this elusive sound has a phonetic symbol all to itself, it is generally agreed that it comes close to sounding like the 'u' in 'cup'. As well as this, believe it or not, there are silent vowels that are not pronounced at all as in the last syllable of 'season'.

CONSONANTS

Consonants are more varied and complicated than vowels and there are far more letters in our alphabet to represent them. Even so, there are not enough letters to indicate accurately all the consonant sounds.

As with vowels, consonants are nearly always made with egressive air and many of them are voiceless and do not involve the vocal cords. Most of the voiceless consonants can be paired with a voiced counterpart, an obvious example being 'S' and 'Z'. 'S' and 'Z' could be described as being identical except that 'Z' is voiced and 'S' is not. Otherwise, the action is exactly the same. However, if you compare the degree of activity of these two consonants, you will find that 'S' requires more force than 'Z'. This is characteristic of all the paired consonants: the unvoiced ones are strong and the voiced ones are weaker because the voicing greatly impedes the airflow. You can frighten a cat with an 'S' but you are unlikely to do so with a 'Z'.

These paired consonants are attractively named fortis (strong) and lenis (gentle) and I think it is worthwhile to compare some of them. Try them for yourself but remember not to say the letters by name e.g. TEE, DEE, but to make the sound as when they are part of a word.

FORTIS		LENIS	
T	as in toot	D	as in did
P	as in pop	B	as in Bob
K	as in kick	G	as in gag
CH	as in church	J	as in judge
F	as in fat	V	as in vat
S	as in Sue	Z	as in zoo
SH	as in shut	S*	as in vision
TH*	as in thought	TH*	as in though

[* These are typical examples of the inadequacies of our alphabet: there is no specific letter to indicate the particular sound of the middle consonant of the word 'vision' which also occurs in decision, division, leisure, azure and many other words. It is neither an 'S' nor a 'Z' but similar to the French 'J' as in 'je'. In the same way, there is nothing in the spelling to differentiate between the pronunciation of one 'TH' and the other; we just have to listen to other people and assume that they are right.

The rest of the consonants do not belong to what is known as the fortis/lenis correlation. Those remaining are 'H', the three nasal consonants 'M', 'N' and 'NG', 'L' and 'R', the two semi-vowels 'Y' and 'W', and the elusive 'WH'.]

H

As a consonant, 'H' is very much on its own because it does not require the involvement of the tongue except to anticipate a vowel - the 'H' of 'heart' is different from the 'H' of 'heat', for instance. A pure 'H', if there is such a thing, is a gentle friction passing through a relatively open throat. An example of this is when you breathe on a mirror or frozen window pane to polish it. A certain amount of effort is required to produce an 'H' but not so much as to sound like clearing the throat. This effort is too much for some people and the result is 'dropped H's' which can be very much looked down on, certainly in England, in spite of the fact that even educated people drop them occasionally. Some uneducated individuals, mindful of the stigma of 'dropped H's', will make such an effort as to put them in the wrong place and will come out with phrases like 'The hatmosphere in 'ere is 'orrible'.

There are, of course, a few words in English, mostly derived from the French, where the 'H' is 'officially' dropped as in 'hour' and 'heiress'. 'H' should be respected and awarded its due and proper place.

M, N, NG

These are the three nasal consonants, so called because the mouth is blocked and the soft palate lowered so that the vibrating airflow escapes through the nose.

    M   where the lips seal the mouth
    N   where the mouth is open but the tongue is raised, sealing it off

NG   in words like 'sing', where the back of the tongue is raised against the lowered soft palate.

L, R

Both 'L' and 'R' are nearly always voiced; they have a variety of possibilities in execution usually dependent on what sound comes before or after. The position of the tongue for 'L' is similar to that of 'N' (the tip touching the alveolar ridge behind the upper teeth) except that the sound can escape laterally over the sides of the tongue. There are at least two distinct ways of pronunciation - the 'clear L' and the 'dark L'.

The 'clear 'L'	The tongue position is fairly high and is typical when the 'L' is followed by a vowel as in 'lip' or 'late'.
The 'dark 'L'	The tongue position is the same at the front but lower in the middle and is typical when the 'L' follows a vowel as in 'hell' or 'roll'

The difference in resonance of the two 'L's' can be clearly felt and heard. On occasion, 'L' is voiceless when it follows 'P', 'T' or 'C' as in 'please', 'quietly' and 'class'.

R

In English, there are several ways of pronouncing 'R'. Most familiar are the 'voiced R', the 'rolled R' and its shorter version the 'one-tap trill'. These will be fully dealt with in the 'R' Factor (P. 162).

As with 'L', there is a 'darker' version of the 'voiced R' which is common in the south west of England, the south of Ireland and the Mid-West and West of the United States. This is the 'retroflexive R' where the tongue tip is pulled quite far back in the mouth, causing a dark continuity of sound. One of the distinguishing features of American speech is that nearly all 'R's' after vowels are noticeably pronounced but differently so according to the region.

According to the American sociolinguist, William Labov, in the Eastern States it is considered to be a sign of social prestige to pronounce the 'R' sound after vowels and that not to pronounce it shows a lower class background. One could say that in England the exact opposite is the case.

In British English, as I stated in the section on phonetics, 'R' following a vowel is usually not pronounced (except in Scotland and some English dialects) but is there to aid the continuance of the vowel it follows, e.g. bird, floor, hard, etc. In a word like 'iron' it doesn't even do that.

When you consider that 'R', besides the above variations, also has completely different pronunciations in French, German, Italian and Spanish, it emerges as a remarkably versatile consonant. Even so, some people have a lot of trouble with it. If you are one of them consult the 'Lazy R' section (P. 164).

W and Y

Both 'W' and 'Y' are better regarded as vowels because, as consonants, they make little or no sound at all. Anyone trying to enunciate either of them purely as a consonant will find themselves forcing their jaw down suddenly to little avail. In the colourful parlance of phonetics they are known as vocalic glides, which doesn't mean much if we don't know what we are sliding from or to. However, once we realize that 'W' is really a short 'OO' sliding to the vowel following, the matter is simple. The word 'we' is easy and clear if pronounced as

'OO+EE'. Similarly, 'will' and 'wet' are pronounced as
'OO+ILL' and 'OO+ET'. In normal conversation, of course,
the 'OO' is very short.

  • Say the following words, starting each one with
  a definite 'OO' and sliding to the vowel after it.
  Where the following vowel happens to be 'OO', as
  in 'womb', you should find yourself automatically
  colouring the first 'OO' slightly differently:
  WE WET WAY WAG WALK WOE WANT WIND
  WINE WORD WOULD WOMB

  • Try also a few words where 'W' is inside the word:
  SWIFT (SOO+IFT) SWEET (SOO+EET)
  ROWING (ROE+OO+ING)
  DRAWING (DRAW+OO+ING)
  COWER (CAH+OO+ER)

'Y' is similar to 'W' in that it is best pronounced as a vowel
— in this case 'EE'. This is very apparent in French
where the name Yves is pronounced Eve. In English,
words like 'yes' and 'you' sound better pronounced as
'EE+ES' and 'EE+OO' but again, in normal speech the
'EE' is very short.

  • Say the following words starting each one with
  a definite 'EE' and sliding to the vowel after it.
  Where the following vowel happens to be 'EE', as
  in 'year', again you should find yourself colouring
  the first 'EE' slightly differently:
  YEAR YET YEA YAP YARD YAWN YOGA YOU
  YEARN YIDDISH YACHT YOUNG
  • Try also a couple of words where the 'Y' is inside
  the word:
  BUYER (BAH+EE+ER) LAWYER (LAW+EE+ER)

Practising 'W' and 'Y' like this will save a lot of ugly
banging down of the jaw.

W and WH

I call 'WH' the 'aspirated W' because, unlike the 'vocalic glide W' described above, it requires some breath to blow it through the lips. This particular sound tends either to be ignored and pronounced as an ordinary 'W' or it is overdone and sounds absurd. In phonetic terms the 'H' is put in front of the 'W' but I think this makes it sound heavy and cumbersome. The best way, I have found, is to prefix the 'W' with a brief, light blow through rounded lips. The ensuing 'OO' and vocalic glide should then move swiftly onto the main vowel.

• Compare the pronunciation of the following pairs of words, remembering to prefix the right-hand column with a short, sharp blow through rounded lips:

WEAR	WHERE
WITCH	WHICH
WET	WHET
WATT	WHAT
WEAL	WHEEL
'Y'	WHY
WIT	WHIT
WILE	WHILE
WAY	WHEY
WEATHER	WHETHER
WALES	WHALES

TH and TH

'TH', either voiced or aspirated, can be a problem, especially for those whose native tongue is not English. For both versions, the tip of the tongue should protrude visibly between the upper and lower teeth.

Consonants, like vowels, can also be placed together in groups of various numbers which are known as consonant clusters. These will be considered later on.

Diction and Articulation

Diction, from the Latin means 'word', and the dictionaries are full of them. However, over the years, diction has come to be interpreted much more to be the manner or pronunciation of speech, whether good or bad. There is good diction and there is bad diction.

When somebody is described as having good, or clear diction we assume that all their words are clearly defined, that each vowel and consonant is correctly judged and that the result is clearly heard. When diction is bad it is generally the consonants that have not been given their full worth and this has given rise to the slight misconception that diction is mostly to do with consonants. Consequently, certain people, worried by remarks about their poor diction, will hammer home their consonants to such a degree that their speech sounds like a firing range. And it usually makes them spit a lot! But shabby vowels can equally be the cause of blurred speech , though this is not so common. Consonants are harder work than vowels which is probably why so many people say 'yeh' instead of 'yes'.

Articulation is another word bandied about by elocutionists as they abjure their pupils to click along their speech like so many clocks.

Articulation is the use of joints; an articulated truck is jointed so that it can negotiate sharp corners. Words are articulated if they have more than one segment. As we have seen in the section on vowels and consonants, the number of segments in a word does not always correspond to the number of letters or syllables. The 5 letter word 'cease' has one syllable but 3 segments 'S' 'EE' 'S' — the first being identical to the last. To emphasize how clear each segment should be, you have only to change the final segment to 'Z' and you have a completely different word, 'sieze'. The 3 syllable word 'multiple' has 8 letters but 7 segments, the final 'e' being silent, each segment requiring a different position of tongue and/or lips. The action of getting from one position to another is articulation, which should be neat and efficient.

A great pianist once said that playing notes was relatively simple. The difficulty lay in the action necessary between the notes. That explains articulation very well, I think. Good articulation means clear diction which, with good tone, means that you will be heard and, provided you are speaking the same language as your audience, in terms they are familiar with, you will be understood. In order to acquire good diction, the first thing you need to consider is the state of your jaw.

JAW AWARENESS

A stiff jaw is one of the most common faults and it can seriously impair the quality of an otherwise good voice. Yet few people know whether they have a stiff jaw or not, and without realizing it, may even find comfort in it and lean on it as though leaning on a bar.

Tension in the jaw can stem from many causes. Being told to shut up, when a child, can be the start of a habit that is hard to break. Determination and aggression can also stiffen up the jaw, often making it jut forward.

Timidity and shyness can equally be the cause of jaw tension, sometimes making it pull back.

It is not at all easy to ascertain yourself whether your jaw is free from tension; it really requires someone else to get hold of your chin so as to move your jaw up and down for you. They will soon know if it is stiff whereas, if you do it yourself, you will probably move your jaw from within instead of letting your hand do it. If you can really let go of your jaw, because that is what it is, another person can manipulate it like an inanimate object. However, many is the time when I have tried to move peoples' jaws when they have hung on to it as a dog hangs on to a bone.

I don't advocate a great deal of exercise for the jaw because it gets quite enough from eating and a lot of exercise could make it stiffer. What is more important is to explore its mobility; to let go of it and find its natural drop. In preparation for the following jaw explorations I suggest you go through the loosening processes for the neck, jaw and shoulders first (P. 69).

LETTING GO OF YOUR JAW

> • Sit comfortably on an upright chair and be conscious that the back muscles of your neck are holding your head well out of your shoulders. Try to feel that you are one of the lucky people whose jaw *is* loose. If this is so, and your jaw is at its natural drop, you should, with your lips closed, be able to run your tongue all the way round between your upper and lower teeth. If your tongue cannot get between them, because they are clenched or touching, then a certain amount of tension must be holding your jaw up.
> • Keeping your lips lightly together, adopt a

strong chewing motion. After a few chews, keep your jaw in the down, extended position for a moment and then relax it. Your jaw should float up to about half way leaving a gap between your upper and lower teeth wide enough to run your tongue all the way round. This is what I call the jaw repose level.

• Get hold of your chin with your thumb and forefinger and see if your jaw will move up and down. If it does, make sure the hand is moving the jaw and that the jaw is not anticipating the hand and moving itself. Try this a few times.

• Place the back of your hand just below your dropped chin. Then, hardly giving it a thought, flick your hand up so that it makes the jaw close. If it is loose it will fly up and make a satisfying 'clomp' against your top teeth. Let it relax down and do it again (keep you tongue well out of the way and be careful of any crowns.) Don't let the jaw anticipate what the hand is going to do. Try to imagine somebody else is doing it to you or, indeed, *let* somebody else do it to you. Do it several times and then do it making a vocal sound through it – even speaking through it – keeping the speaking independent of the jaw movement.

It is well worth getting this right, so I recommend alternating it with the following more unusual procedures.

JAW LOOSENERS

• Relax your jaw so that it drops to repose level then, very gently, move it from side to side without forcing. You will find this is not possible

unless your jaw is at its natural drop or your
bottom teeth will scrape unpleasantly across
your top teeth. Your lips should be slightly apart.
When you have done this a few times and found
it easy, try moving the jaw forwards and back
wards, without forcing. A mere fraction is enough
to prove that the jaw is not a fixed entity.

• Now return to the gentle, side to side movement
and try saying something as you do so. Some
thing simple like, "Hello, there. How are you?" Try
to time the movement against the rhythm of the
words so that you feel the disinvolvement of the
jaw. When you have tried this a few times it
should be easy. Saying something like, "Good
morning, my dear." will seem slightly more difficult because the lips will be chasing each other in
order to come together for the two 'm's'. Even so,
it is possible to do and is very beneficial.

We have seen from the above movements that the jaw
can be in several places other than the generally accepted ones but it is of paramount importance for
speech clarity that it is in the right place at the right
time. And where is that, you might say? Certainly, it is
rarely out of place laterally, for that would interfere with
the 'bite', but quite often with some people the jaw is too
far back — occasionally it is too far forward but this is
rare — and the habit of a lifetime can make the wrong
position feel right and the right position feel wrong.

T-13

• Try this experiment: ease your jaw forward as
far as it will comfortably go (kids do this when
they are pretending to be animals or Dracula).
Now, say something ordinary like, "It's a lovely
day, today."

The speech will sound and feel peculiar. However, your

larynx will be free and your throat will be open but the focus will be lost at the front.

> • Now, pull your jaw in a fraction and say "It's a lovely day today" again. Repeat the phrase, gradually pulling in your jaw each time, until you feel the focus of the words is clear. At this point, make a mental note of where your lower incisors are in relation to your upper incisors.
> • Now, pull your jaw inwards into the 'chinless wonder' position and again say, "It's a lovely day, today."

This will sound even more peculiar because the uncomfortable compression on the larynx and throat will cramp the tone and again the frontal focus is lost.

> • From pulled back position, ease your jaw forward a fraction and say the phrase again. Repeat it, easing your jaw forward each time until you feel the focus of the words is clear. Again, make a mental note of where your lower incisors are in relation to your upper incisors.

It is most likely that your voice will sound at its best when your lower incisors are directly under your upper incisors. You can judge the results much better if you record yourself on tape. Now us let us capitalize on the jaw position we used in the 'Whispered HA's' (P.80).

> • Relax your jaw so that it drops to the repose level check that the back teeth are apart — then slowly and gently ease your jaw forward until your lower incisors are more or less directly under your upper upper incisors. Try quickly nipping your front teeth together to test this. (A few people may have to move their jaw back into the teeth-matching position.)

• Let your jaw drop to repose level without falling back and let your lips smile gently over this position. It should look extremely good. Hold this position as still as possible, without stiffening and, letting your tongue and lips move freely round this ideal space, again say, "It's a lovely day, today," taking especial care to resonate the 'l's' in 'lovely'. It should sound very clear and pleasant. Check in the mirror that the jaw hardly moves, except for a gentle rise and fall for the 'v' in 'lovely', and that the teeth remain apart about the width of a pencil.

• Slide a pencil or similar object crossways between your teeth or the tip of a finger and say: "It's a lovely day, today" several times, making sure that your tongue and lips move freely and independently.

• Repeat the phrase, and any other phrase you care to use, alternating with the pencil or your finger between your teeth, and then without, but holding the same position. You will soon know what it is to speak with a free jaw.

When your jaw is free we can begin to consider your tongue.

TONGUE AWARENESS

The tongue easily gets involved in the business of other organs' work. For instance, it *will* involve itself in the breathing process, where it has no part to play, and this will trigger off a chain of unwanted tensions. Our first task is to separate the tongue from breathing movements.

• Let your jaw drop so that your mouth is

pleasantly open. Take a long, deep breath and watch in the mirror that your tongue does not move backwards with it. Similarly, when you breathe out, watch that your tongue does not move up. Keep the front of your tongue gently touching the back of your lower teeth.

• Repeat these breaths several times, watching the front of your throat, and check that your larynx (Adam's apple) does not move down when breathing in. If it does, it means that either your tongue is pressing down on your larynx or the larynx itself is not sufficiently open to allow the breath in with ease. Make sure you open your throat to welcome the breath in; do not filter it through tense muscles. If your larynx does not move down when you breathe in it should have no need to rise when you breathe out.

Try to get used to the feeling that you can breathe in and out *over* the tongue without involving it. Don't, however, stiffen it in any way to keep it still. Just don't use it.

• Prove to yourself even further that the tongue can be independent by putting it out on your bottom lip and breathing in and out in a gentle panting. See that it does not move. Try the tongue even further out (rather like a dog) and do the panting quicker and smaller — like a flicker. The tongue shouldn't even *want* to move!

TONGUE LOOSENERS

1. Open your mouth fairly wide as though for an enthusiastic smile and poke your tongue out straight ahead to a comfortable extension then let it relax back into your mouth again. The effort should only be in the push out, not the

pulling in. Repeat this shuttle-like movement
and check with thumb and finger that the larynx
doesn't move.

T-14

2. Gently lodge the tip of your tongue behind your
bottom front teeth and, in your normal speaking
voice, slowly alternate the two sounds 'EE' and
'AH' several times. Try them detached at first:
EE AH EE AH EE AH EE AH then join them up in
a smooth continuation: EE-AH-EE-AH-EE-AH,
checking in the mirror that the jaw does not move
but remains uninvolved. The tip of your tongue
should be anchored while the middle should rise
forwards on 'EE' and fall back again on 'AH'.
Again, check that the larynx does not move up
and down.

3. At an easy pace repeat: EE-AH-EE-AH-EE-AH-
EE-AH-EE-AH. First, whispered and then with
the voice. *Breathe in to commence.*

Whisper: EE-AH-EE-AH-EE-AH-EE-AH-EE-AH
                (1   2   3   4   5)
Voice: EE-AH-EE-AH-EE-AH-EE-AH-EE-AH
Repeat several times, alternating the voice with
the whisper.

4. After several repetitions, with the tongue nicely
shuttling back and forth,the voice should sound
much freer. Let the result echo round your face.

5. Try exactly the same thing at double the speed.
This will sound more like: YA-YA-YA-YA-YA-YA-
YA-YA-YA

Whisper: YA-YA-YA-YA-YA-YA-YA-YA-YA
                (1 2 3 4 5 6 7 8 9)
Voice: YA-YA-YA-YA-YA-YA-YA-YA-YA

(I give the number of nine repetitions as a form of decision making and it is a convenient number. You can do more or less but it is better to decide before you begin.)

6. With the same mouth position, exercise the back of the tongue, using a string of 'GA's':

Whisper: GA-GA-GA-GA-GA-GA-GA-GA-GA
        (1 2 3 4 5 6 7 8 9)
Voice: GA-GA-GA-GA-GA-GA-GA-GA-GA

then try a string of 'KA's':

Whisper: KA-KA-KA-KA-KA-KA-KA-KA-KA
        (1 2 3 4 5 6 7 8 9)
Voice: KA-KA-KA-KA-KA-KA-KA-KA-KA

This is an extension of the exercise for loosening the Throat Muscles (P. 72)

7. Now exercise the *front* of your tongue by comparing the two consonants, 'T' and 'D':
TEE-TEE-TEE-TEE and DEE-DEE-DEE-DEE

Check in the mirror that the tip of your tongue is up for the 'T' and the 'D' but down for the 'EE'. Do not move your jaw.

8. Alternate 'T' and 'D' slowly: TEE-DEE-TEE-DEE-TEE-DEE. Don't do this too quickly or the TEE will get more and more like the DEE which is minimally easier to perform. (American pronunciation often substitutes 'D' for 'T'.)

9. Alternate 'THEE' and 'TEE', and 'THEE' and 'DEE'. For 'THEE' make sure your tongue loosely protrudes under your top teeth. Pull it in again for 'TEE' and 'DEE'.

10. Compare the voiced and aspirated'TH', e.g. THESE THINGS — your tongue protruding for *both* versions!

11. The tongue roll: Take a long breath and return it at once into your mouth to produce a whirring sound with your tongue against the hard ridge behind your top teeth. Very like a drum roll, this is the movement that constitutes the so-called 'rolled R' (P. 163 and P. 166) .

As well as 'T' and 'D', 'N' is also good for exercising the blade or tip of the tongue. Notice in the following exercises how it flicks up and down.

12. Drop your jaw to its repose level so that your upper and lower teeth are about a pencil width apart. Without moving your jaw, repeat the following sounds in groups of four. Join up the four repetitions into one continuous sound. That way you will also get a build-up of nasal resonance:
NEE-NEE-NEE-NEE   NAY-NAY-NAY-NAY
NAH-NAH-NAH-NAH   NO-NO-NO-NO
NOO-NOO-NOO-NOO

13. Alternate NEE with each of the others:

NEE-NAY-NEE-NAY-NEE-NAY-NEE-NAY
NEE-NAH-NEE-NAH-NEE-NAH-NEE-NAH
NEE-NO-NEE-NO-NEE-NO-NEE-NO
NEE-NOO-NEE-NOO-NEE-NOO-NEE-NOO

14. Try a triple effect:

NEE-NAY-NAH-NEE-NAY-NAH-NEE-NAY-NAH
NEE-NAY-NO-NEE-NAY-NO-NEE-NAY-NO
NEE-NAY-NOO-NEE-NAY-NOO-NEE-NAY-NOO

15. Then all five in succession:

NEE-NAY-NAH-NO-NOO

The permutations are endless.

16. Repeat the last few exercises, substituting 'L' for 'N'. Drop your jaw a little further to allow more space for the greater movement of your tongue. Check in the mirror that you don't move your jaw to articulate the 'L's'. If necessary try it first with two fingertips between your teeth (making a double width). The lateral resonance should be less nasal than for 'N'.

LEE-LEE-LEE-LEE   LAY-LAY-LAY-LAY
LAH-LAH-LAH-LAH   LO-LO-LO-LO-LO
LOO-LOO-LOO-LOO

17. The triple effect:

LEE-LAY-LAH-LEE-LAY-LAH-LEE-LAY-LAH
LEE-LAY-LO-LEE-LAY-LO-LEE-LAY-LO
LEE-LAY-LOO-LEE-LAY-LOO-LEE-LAY-LOO

18. Then all five:

LEE-LAY-LAH-LO-LOO

19. Alternate using the tip with the back of the tongue and compare the two sensations when saying:

TICK-TICK-TICK-TICK

Make sure that only your tongue moves and that your jaw remains still.

20. Then exaggerate the final 'K' sound until it acquires a neutral vowel — in British English I would spell it as 'TICKER' but I don't want the 'R' pronounced, as this pulls the tongue back and slows things down. Without the 'R' you can work up quite a speed with:

TICKER-TICKER-TICKER-TICKER-TICKER-TICKER-TICKER etc.

21. Alternate using the back of the tongue with the tip:

GUH-DUH-GUH-DUH-GUH-DUH-GUH-DUH
or:
GIDDY-GIDDY-GIDDY-GIDDY-GIDDY-GIDDY

WORDS TO TRY

Front of the tongue: tat, tot, toot, tatty, dad, did, dud, deed, dude, dotty, ditty, duty, dirty, teddy, tidy, etiquette, institute, these, theatres etc.

Front and middle: deal, dole, dial, lit, let, deleted, delighted, lily, lolly, truly, trolley, trial, trail, told, dandy, land, loaned etc.

Back of the tongue: gag, keg, cog, coke, could kick, guy, agog, ago etc.

Various combinations: tag, dug, gun, get, gate, god, dog, giddy, good, gold, greet, great, tick-tock, clock, track, trick, kit, cut, kicked, knick-knack, knuckle, gargantuan, garden, goggle, ganglion, tittle-tattle, other, thought, ethnic etc.

SOFT PALATE AWARENESS

Controlling a wayward soft palate is not easy because there is so little sensation in it. Sometimes it will not lift when we want it to and various ruses have to be employed to 'trick' it into action.

> • Open your mouth fairly wide as though you are going to laugh; leave your tongue loosely flat, especially at the back and flex your soft palate upwards into an arch. Check in the mirror; it should look like this:

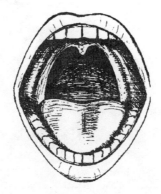

Figure 24: Soft Palate Up

You should be able to see the back wall of your pharynx through the arch of the raised soft palate.

> • If your soft palate refuses to budge, try the yawn position without actually yawning. If this fails, imagine a fish-bone lodged between your tongue as soft palate or think what it feels like when you vomit. These last two are rather an effort but are very effective for singers with lazy soft palates. Perhaps the best way is to imagine you are smiling with the back of your mouth. In any case, persevere until you achieve the look in the diagram.

At this point, we should not ignore the uvula, the soft, fleshy appendage that hangs down from the middle of the soft palate. Some are longer than others which means a little more effort because if it is left to drag on the tongue it can cause an unpleasant gutteral rattle.

> • Having lifted the soft palate off the back of your tongue, beware of raising it too high or it will seal off the top of the pharynx and the nasal cavity. This also tends to pull the tonsil pillars in and reduces the amount of sound passing into the mouth.

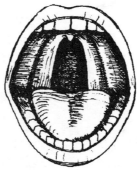

Figure 25: Tonsil Pillars Too Far In

In short, the ideal position for the soft palate is mid-way between the oral cavity and the naso-pharynx. Once you are able to lift your soft palate (and uvula) into an arch similar to that in Figure 24, here is a good way of finding just where that position is:

> • With your mouth fairly wide open, look in the mirror and see that your soft palate is well arched. Take an easy, deep breath and quietly say 'AH'. Check in the mirror that your tongue and soft palate barely move but remain uninvolved. This can be quite a challenge but it is well worth the trouble. It helps to feel that you are keeping everything out of the way to make way for

the breath to go in and the sound to come out. Do
rest between efforts.

• Look into your mouth with the mirror again
and, with the soft palate arched at the back, say
'AH'. It should sound quite clear. Now, still look
ing in the mirror, bring the soft palate and the
tongue together, blocking off the mouth, and say
'AH' again. This time it will sound muffled and
indistinguishable. As mentioned before, the nearest spelling for this sound is 'NG'.

• Alternate the 'AH' and the 'NG' several times
and be conscious of the sensation of your tongue
touching your soft palate and separating from it.
The two sounds should be markedly different.

SOFT PALATE LOOSENERS

1. Say a long 'AH' and bring your tongue and soft
palate together and separate them at regular
intervals along the sound.

AH-NG-AH-NG-AH-NG-AH-NG etc.

I have put hyphens to indicate that the sound
should be continuous. The action of the tongue
and soft palate is the same as when you say
'singing' or 'ringing'.

2. Use these ordinary words and extend them;
feel what it is like to say 'singing' and then repeat
it with several more 'ings' added:

SINGING   SINGINGINGINGINGINGINGING
SANG   SANGANGANGANGANGANGANG
SONG   SONGONGONGONGONGONG
SUNG   SUNGUNGUNGUNGUNGUNG

You can try it with other vowels like 'ENG', 'AWNG' and 'OONG'. Like the 'MUH-NUH-MUH-NUH's', there should be a continuous resonance above the articulations.

As you can see, the soft palate works very much in conjunction with the tongue, not only for the 'NG' sound but also for 'G' and 'K'. Try 'G' and 'K' in front of some of the main vowels. Where there is a question of pronunciation the word at the end will give the clue. Keep your jaw as still as possible during the repetitions:

3. GHEE-GHEE-GHEE - GEYSER   KEE-KEE-KEE - KEY
    GHI-GHI-GHI - GIVE   KI-KI-KI - KICK
    GHe-GHe-GHe - GET   Ke-Ke-Ke - KEPT
    Ga-Ga-Ga - GAS   Ka-Ka-Ka - CASH
    GAH-GAH-GAH - GARDEN   KAH-KAH-KAH -CAR
    GU-GU-GU - GUN   KU-KU-KU - COME
    GAW-GAW-GAW - GAUDY   KAW-KAW-KAW - CALL
    GO-GO-GO - GOAL   KO-KO-KO - COAL
    Go-Go-Go - GONE   Ko-Ko-ko - COMIC
    GOO-GOO-GOO - GOOSE   KOO-KOO-KOO - COOL
    Goo-Goo-Goo - GOOD   Koo-Koo-Koo - COULD
    GHER-GHER--GHERKIN   KER-KER-- CURTAIN

4. Now try the G and the K <u>after</u> a selection of vowels:

EEG-EEG- EAGRE   EEK-EEK-EEK - ECONOMIC
IG-IG-IG - IGNORANT   eK-eK-eK - EXTRA
eG-eG-eG - EGG   aK-aK-aK - ACTOR
aG-aG-aG - AGONY   AHK-AHK-AHK - ARCHIVE
AHG-AHG-AHG - ARGUE   UK-UK-UK - UXBRIDGE
UG-UG-UG - UGLY   AWK-AWK-AWK - AWKWARD
AWG-AWG-AWG -AUGUST   OK-OK-OK - OAK
OG-OG-OG - OGRE   oK-oK-oK - OCTOBER
ERG-ERG- ERGONOMIC   ERK-ERK- IRKSOME

These are just helpful examples. There is nothing to stop you thinking up some of your own.

5. Use two vowels which are formed at the back of the mouth - OO, the highest tongue position, and 'AH', the lowest tongue position. Prefix them with 'G' and feel the contrast in space; 'GOO' should feel almost closed while 'GAH' should feel wide open once the vowel has been reached, a pleasant relief, in fact:

GOO-GOO-GOO-GOO-GAH
GOO-GOO-GOO-GOO-GAH etc.

6. Try it at various pitches with only passive involvement of the front of your tongue. The tip should remain as near to the back of your lower incisors as possible.

7. Gradually elongate the GAH:

GOO-GOO-GOO-GOO-GAH
GOO-GOO-GOO-GOO-GAAH
GOO-GOO-GOO-GOO-GAAAH
GOO-GOO-GOO-GOO-GAAAAH etc.

While this could equally be considered an exercise for the back of the tongue, it underlines the relationship of the tongue with the soft palate.

CONSCIOUS USE OF YOUR HARD PALATE

The hard palate and the alveolar ridge are fixtures that cannot be improved with exercise or re-positioning. We can, however, make ourselves much more conscious in our use of them.

The tongue, as we have observed, articulates against the alveolar ridge a great deal, particularly with the consonants, 'T', 'D', 'L' and 'N'. As well as this, all the vowels which are formed in the front of the mouth, such as 'EE', 'eh' (as in BED), 'AIR' (a diphthong) and 'ă' (as in BAD), are identifiable by the distance between the alveolar ridge and the tongue - not the tip of the tongue but the *bend* in the tongue as can be seen in Figures 18-19-20.

T-15

• For instance, say these four major vowels which are formed at the front of the mouth:

EE   (as in BEAD)
eh   (as in BED)
AIR   (as in BARED)
ă   (as in BAD)

For 'EE', there should be a small space between your upper and lower teeth but, as you progress through the other vowels, your jaw should open wider and your tongue should be increasingly further away from the alveolar ridge. In the phonetics vowel scale the four sounds are represented as being equidistant apart; if precise measurements could be given, one could say that the space between the upper and lower teeth for 'EE' should be a quarter of an inch; for 'eh' it should be half an inch; for 'AIR' it should be three-quarters of an inch and for 'ă' it should be an inch. Although these proportions are a bit on the generous side, it does make the ratio clear.

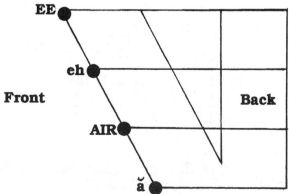

Figure 26: The Four Front Vowels

As far as tone is concerned, the actual hard palate or roof of your mouth is a vital sounding-board for singing or speaking and your main task, in this respect, is to be able to aim your voice at it. I cannot stress this too forcefully: unless the voice is aimed successfully at this little piece of equipment so that it reverberates, its carrying power and audibility will be seriously impaired. Because the hard palate is so hard and is situated between two spaces, it has the ability to give the voice "ping", making it as bright and clear as a microphone can. You might well ask how one does this aiming and I can only say by trial and error. I am a great believer in trying things several ways until you hit the right spot.

> 1. Let your head drop back onto your collar so that your mouth is left open and your tongue is loosely flat. Check in the mirror that you can see the roof of your mouth and that your soft palate is raised.

> 2. Take a deep breath and bring it back on a good, firm 'HA', bouncing it off the hard palate straight out of your mouth.

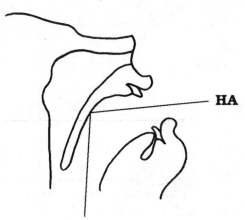

Figure 27: HA off the Hard Palate

3. Try the 'HA' three times on one breath and bounce the sound off the hard palate as sound bounces off a wall.

4. Now, as a contrast, try bouncing the 'HA' off your soft palate.

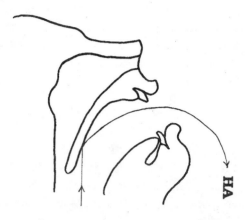

Figure 28: HA off the Soft Palate

The result will be muffled as there is very little rebound off soft, movable surfaces.

5. Aim at the hard palate again, making sure the soft palate is sufficiently raised to let the voice through. It should have a good "ping" but not be hard.

6. Finally, alternate the hard palate 'HA' with the soft palate 'HA' several times and be aware of the difference.

One more important point about the hard palate is when it is vibrating, it can send reverberations up into the nasal cavity of which it is the floor, and upwards and forwards into the nasal sinuses and skull. This is what makes the voice carry, naturally, in large rooms and small.

LIP AWARENESS

In the old days of elocution great store was set on lip
exercises as a means of ensuring clear speech. However,
over-use of the lips when speaking is frankly worse than
under-use.

Busy, exaggerated lip movements not only distort speech
but they are very wearing for those listeners having to
look at them. Even those deaf people who are good at lip
reading are confused when words are too 'mouthed'.
Over-mouthing words to a deaf person is as pointless as
shouting your own language at foreigners to make them
understand.

Under-use of the lips can also be irritating. The commonest form of this is the 'frozen' upper lip. True, the
upper lip is far less mobile than the lower lip, but not to
use it at all robs the speech of precision and liveliness.
A top lip that always lies flat on the upper teeth somehow
acts as a mute on the vocal resonance. I can think of one
TV news reader who suffers from this with the result that
her speech sounds dull and wooden — even the good
news sounds bad.

The golden rule for lips is to use them no more than
enough. For instance, it is quite possible to say 'cha-
cha-cha' without moving the lips at all. Try it and you'll
see. Then try it again, letting the lips do what they want
to by slightly rounding outwards on each 'ch', and falling
back in a relaxed state on the 'ah'. To overdo the 'ch'
movement would reduce the speed considerably and it
would look and sound bizarre.

There are at least five basic positions for the lips in
speech though none of them can be described as fixtures.

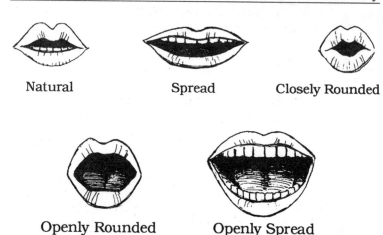

Figure 29: Mouth Positions

Natural (or neutral) for 'ER' 'UH' 'eh'; Spread for 'EE'; Closely Rounded for 'OO'; Openly Rounded for 'OH'; Openly Spread for the 'Big AH'.

In order that the lips can negotiate these positions when called upon, with swiftness and ease, they need to be completely free from tension and as loose as possible.

LIP LOOSENERS

1. Blow breath through loosely closed lips using no voice. The lips should vibrate against each other sounding like a horse blowing down its nose as on page 113.

2. Same as No. 1, only this time use voice. The sounds like the 'Brrr' we say when we are cold.

3. Vigorously shake your head from side to side so that your lips and jowls flop loosely away from

your skull and jaw. Use voice for this but don't try
it if you've got a hangover!

LIP EXERCISES

1. Gently push your lips forward into a pursed or
kiss position, then relax them so that they fall
back to their original position (zero). Do six
repetitions of this.

2. Spread your lips as though smiling, feeling the
cheeks crease up, then relax them so that they
fall back to zero. (When spreading your lips,
check in the mirror that your neck muscles are
not involved. Use only the muscles around your
mouth.)

3. Alternate these two extreme positions - from
the kiss position to the wide smile and back
again. Do six repetitions, which is quite enough.

4. Vocalise the last exercise by saying

OO-EE-OO-EE-OO-EE-OO-EE
OO-EE-OO-EE-OO-EE-OO-EE
making each change of lip position very definite.

5. Bearing in mind that any word beginning with
the letter 'W' should be pronounced as though
beginning with a short 'OO', try 'W' against four
important vowels:

OO-EE = we	OO-EE-OO-EE-OO-EE-OO-EE
OO-AY = way	OO-AY-OO-AY-OO-AY-OO-AY
OO-AW = war	OO-AW-OO-AW-OO-AW-OO-AW
OO-OH = woe	OO-OH-OO-OH-OO-OH-OO-OH

6. 'B', 'P' and 'M' are all 'lip-smackers', 'B' and 'P'

both starting with a small explosion of air (called a plosive in phonetic terms). Try 'B' against five important vowels, each in a continuous sound:

BEE-BEE-BEE-BEE-BEE
BAY-BAY-BAY-BAY-BAY
BAH-BAH-BAH-BAH-BAH
BOH-BOH-BOH-BOH-BOH
BOO-BOO-BOO-BOO-BOO

7. Then do them in rotation, slowly first, then quickly:

BEE-BAY-BAH-BOH-BOO

8. Repeat this whole sequence, substituting 'P' for 'B':

PEE-PEE-PEE-PEE-PEE
PAY-PAY-PAY-PAY-PAY
PAH-PAH-PAH-PAH-PAH
POH-POH-POH-POH-POH
POO-POO-POO-POO-POO
and:
PEE-PAY-PAH-POH-POO

9. Repeat, replacing 'P' with M':

MEE-MEE-MEE-MEE-MEE
MAY-MAY-MAY-MAY-MAY
MAH-MAH-MAH-MAH-MAH
MOH-MOH-MOH-MOH-MOH
MOO-MOO-MOO-MOO-MOO
and:
MEE-MAY-MAH-MOH-MOO

There is no disputing that the bottom lip is far more mobile than the upper lip. You have only to repeat part of the last exercise - using 'M' - looking in the mirror. Say 'MEE-MEE MEE-MEE-MEE' and you will observe that the bottom lip moves down and up at every articulation while the upper lip is almost motionless. No harm in that, but here is an exercise to put some life into the upper lip:

10. Say 'MEE-MEE-MEE-MEE-MEE' fairly slowly, being conscious of *only moving the bottom lip*. Keep a check in the mirror. Now, repeat 'MEE-MEE-MEE-MEE MEE' and *only move the upper lip*. This is difficult at first; it is rather like sneering. Do it really slowly until you can separate the movement of the upper lip from the lower. Practise the following, first with lower lip movement then with upper lip movement:

MEE-MEE-MEE-MEE-MEE
MAY-MAY-MAY-MAY-MAY
MAH-MAH-MAH-MAH-MAH

Persevere with this but don't let it drive you crazy.

11. A good exercise for the bottom lip is to alternate 'F' and 'V' against various vowels. Take care that you do not bite your upper incisors on your bottom lip but bring the lip up slightly in front of them. It is helpful to associate the sounds with suitable words.

FEE - VEE   (feet - visa)
FAY - VAY   (fate - vague)
Fa - Va   (fat - vat)
FAH - VAH   (fast - vast)
FER - VER   (first - virtue)

You could round this exercise of nicely by singing Peggy Lee's famous song, 'Fever'.

The 'R' Factor

As mentioned earlier, 'R' is one of the most versatile consonants and the three options open to us in English are well worth exploring. They are the 'voiced R', the 'rolled R' and the 'one-tap trill'.

T-16

The Voiced R - is the most frequently used 'R' sound. Linguistically known as a 'voiced, frictionless continuant', the vocal tone travels over the tongue which is fairly high in the mouth with the tip (or blade) slightly back from the alveolar ridge. You should find that the sides of the tongue contract a little so that the sound travels down the middle line. The 'voiced R' is most frequently used at the beginning of words and when 'R' follows 'T'.

> • Try the following words with a very pronounced voicing of the 'R's'. In order to do this pull your tongue back a little way in your mouth so that the sides bunch up against your upper molars and the tip is fairly high; pause a moment on each 'R' resonance before releasing your tongue for the rest of the word:
> REAL RICH RARE RAIN RED
> RASH RANCH RAW ROSE ROOM

This retroflexion of the tongue will 'darken' the 'R' and

make you much more aware of it. Then you can repeat
the words letting your tongue take its normal course.

The One-tap trill — otherwise known as the alveolar
flap is a roll consisting of only one tap or flap of the
tongue against the alveolar ridge and is very effective in
making words sound precise or sharp. It is most effective
when following another consonant.

> • Try these words first of all with a voiced 'R' and
> then with a one-tap trill which is like a tiny
> crunch between the first consonant and the
> vowel and see which you prefer:

> CREAK BREATH GRATE SCRAP BRANCH
> FRAUGHT BROKE BRISK PRICK GRIP FRUIT
> ARROW TERROR TOMORROW

The 'one-tap trill' is particularly effective in words where
it follows 'sc', e.g. 'screech', 'script', 'scratch' and 'screw'.

The Rolled R - is similar to a drum-roll, hence its name,
and it is usually indicated in scripts and plays by a string
of 'r's' e.g. 'rrrreally'. It is voiced while the tongue flaps
in a continuous flutter against the alveolar ridge. This
movement is also possible with unvoiced air but then it
is not so much a speech sound. Its use in normal English
tends to sound eccentric though it can be useful for
'special effects'. As an exercise it is invaluable and for
speaking Spanish and Italian it is essential.

> • Try saying 'GRRRR' - the written equivalent of
> a growl. Rolled 'R's' are easiest after consonants
> like 'B', 'C' and 'G', e.g. BRRRRUTE, CRRRRAZY
> and GRRRREEDY.

> • Alternate the unvoiced and voiced 'rolled R'
> without any identifiable vowel.

• Roll the 'R's' onto these vowels:
RRRREE   RRRRAY
RRRRAH   RRRRAW   RRRROH   RRRROO

• Roll the 'R's' onto words like 'really', 'Richard',
'ready', 'random', 'raucous' and 'ruin':
RRRREALLY RRRRICHARD RRRREADY
RRRRANDOM RRRRAUCOUS RRRRUIN

If you are one of those people who can't roll their 'R's',
don't worry. See below.

HOW TO CURE A 'LAZY R'

There are quite a number of people who are unable to say
their 'R's' let alone roll them. This does not always worry
them - Cockneys make a feature of it, so do some English
Lords. It may sound quaint but it really is an unnecessary impediment. In some cases this is caused by the
sub-lingual frenum (that small ligament that acts as a
bridle under the tongue) being too short and preventing
the tongue from lifting up and back. More often though,
I have found it to be the result of bad management or just
plain laziness. It is certainly possible to do something
about it.

T-17

1. Lock the blade of your tongue down behind
your bottom front teeth and say something like
'Rabbits like fresh, crunchy, red radishes'. Feel
what it is like to impede your tongue *purposely*.

2. Repeat several times before releasing your
tongue and saying the phrase unimpeded. Compare the two versions.

3. Pull your tongue back a little way in your
mouth so that the sides bunch up against your
molars and push the tip up as far as you can

towards the hard palate. If your tongue refuses to lift high enough, insert a clean finger under it and ease it upwards.

4. With your tongue held high, make a vocal sound and let it come up through the small space between your tongue and the roof of your mouth. Any sound will do; just let it happen.

5. Repeat this sound behind your tongue and use it as the first part of the word 'arrive'. Elongate this sound a little before letting your tongue flop down for the second syllable. Try the same approach to other similar words; 'arithmetic', 'around', 'arrest'.

6. Now use the sound behind the raised tongue as the 'R' sound initiating these words:
REAL RICH RARE RACK RAFT RAW ROSE ROOF.
Elongate the 'R' sound a little before releasing your tongue for the vowel.

7. As a further challenge to your tongue, repeat the words again with your finger remaining underneath it and providing some resistance. Feel the strength of your tongue pushing your finger forward:
REAL RICH RARE RACK RAFT RAW ROSE ROOF.

8. Repeat the same words immediately without the impediment of your finger. Your tongue should feel like a released prisoner.

ROLLING THE 'R'

Rolling the 'R' is a knack of bringing opposing forces together at the right time, e.g. the breath v. the tongue and the alveolar ridge. Now that your tongue has had a chance to flex itself, you must see if you can get it to make the whirring sound.

> 1. Picture the drum-roll sound in your mind, take a breath and, as you breathe out, bring your tongue up and slightly back to compress the air-stream against the roof of your mouth. In this air-stream the blade of your tongue should oscillate against the alveolar ridge.

> 2. Sometimes it is easier to roll the 'R' when the voice is already vibrating as in 'arrive'. This time start the word with your tongue lying slack in the middle of your mouth and bring it sharply up and slightly back to engage with the alveolar ridge; try to roll the 'R's' like mad:

> ARRRRIVE ARRRRITHMETIC ARRRROUND ARRRREST etc.

> 3. If you are still having difficulty, try to do the 'rolled R' sound with your finger under your tongue — it won't work, I can assure you, but remove your finger and try again and it might. It's very like starting a car: when it's cold it won't start but you keep trying and suddenly it does. Cheers!

For those who have always been unable to roll their 'R's', suddenly to be able to do them gives them a great buzz, as they say.

✳

The 'S' Factor

For a pleasant 'S' sound, the upper and lower teeth should be fairly close together and the blade of the tongue should be in complete contact with the alveolar ridge except for the crease down the middle line through which the breath passes. Sometimes the tip of the tongue lightly touches the back of the lower incisors. If the teeth are too far apart the 'S' becomes a lisp, so that instead of 'yes' we get 'yeth', or 'Thaturday' instead of 'Saturday'.

The 'S' sound is pure breath with no voice. Because of the narrowing (or stricture) made by the tongue against the alveolar ridge it is much slower than releasing breath on say, an 'H'. As such, it is an ideal way of monitoring breath as it is released and it can be prolonged as long as one likes before 'switching on' the voice for a vowel or changing to another consonant.

My favourite sentence for practising 'S's' could have been written by the Brothers Grimm:

> • "Six sisters sat on a stone to consider the seriousness of the situation."

> • Read the sentence through out loud and then repeat it doubling or trebling the length of the 'S's'. Keep the sibilance easy and unforced and try to enjoy delaying the 'S' before it transforms into the next sound:

SSSIKSSS SSSISSSTERS SSSAT ON A SSSTONE
TO CONSSSIDER THE SSSERIOUSSSNESSS OF
THE SSSITUATION.

• Using the same principle, prefix these vowels
with the long 'S':
SSSSER SSSSEE SSSSAY SSSSAH SSSSAW
SSSSOH SSSSOO SSSSUH

'S' combines with at least ten other consonant sounds
without losing its identity. To pronounce as many as
possible of them in combination with a variety of vowels
is a pleasant vocal marathon. The discipline is that each
'S' should be identical and slightly elongated before the
rest of the word follows:

• SKI SKID SKETCH SCAN SCAR SCUD SCOTCH
SCORE SCHOOL SKIRT
• SCREECH SCRIPT SCRATCH SCRIBE SCRUB
SCRAWNY SCRUPLE
• SLEEP SLIP SLEPT SLAP SLOT SLAW SLOW
SLEW SLUR
• SMITH SMELL SMACK SMART SMALL
SMOTE SMOOTH
•SNEEZE SNIP SNARE SNATCH SNARL SNUFF
SNORE SNOW SNOOZE
• SQUEEZE SQUID SQUARE SQUAT SQUAW
SQUIRT
• SPEECH SPIT SPEND SPA SPUD SPOT
SPORE SPOKE SPOOK SPURT
•SPREE SPRING SPREAD SPRANG SPRUNG
SPRAWL SPRUCE
• STEAM STICK STAIR STACK STAR STUD STOCK
STORE STOKE STOOL
• STREAM STRICT STRESS STRAP STRUT STRAW
STROKE STREW
• SWEET SWIM SWEAT SWAGGER SWUNG
SWORE SWOLLEN SWOON

'S' combined with 'H' produces a different kind of sound — a single phoneme — which, on its own, seems to have found its way into the vocabulary as meaning "Keep quiet". Comparing 'S' and 'SH' is a useful exploration which will be dealt with in the next section.

HOW TO CURE A HISSING 'S'

Most of those who have this problem are not aware of it themselves but it is very irritating when heard by others and could act as a shibboleth to prospective employer. The over-sibilant 'S' has an amazing carrying power and sometimes is all you can hear of a conversation across a room. Those who are aware that they have this problem usually don't know what to do about it and try to inhibit the 'S', in effect pulling it back, which makes the hiss even worse.

The cause is often a deep-rooted psychological one, allied to shyness and insecurity which in turn causes tension in the lips and tongue. Together with tension in the jaw, this distorts the necessary stricture for 'S' and makes it too high and intense. It is perfectly possible to say 'S's' at various pitches and you should try them but the one we need for speaking is somewhere in the middle. To achieve this there are three factors to remember: 1. the lips are not involved at all; 2. the jaw position must be correct; 3. the tongue position must be correct. These factors can only be adjusted by trial and error so a tape recorder is helpful if you are working by yourself. Make sure you are standing or sitting in a comfortable, upright position and that your neck, jaw and shoulders are free from tension.

Exploring different pitches of 'S':   T-18

    1. Take a good breath and make four 'S' sounds,

the first one as high as possible, the others progressively lower. Repeat this several times and note the difference of stricture for each pitch.

Finding the correct jaw position:

2. Blow air through your closed lips so that they flap loosely. Once loose, make sure they do not tighten up or become involved in any of the following 'S' sounds. Check in the mirror if necessary.

3. Take a good breath and say the word 'cease'. Listen to it on tape if you can and note whether the 'S' sound at the beginning and the end of the word is high and squeaky or not.

4. Pull your jaw back and say 'cease' again and listen. It will sound odd and the pitch will be lower.

5. Ease your jaw as far forward as it will go so that the lower incisors are jutting out. Say 'cease' again and listen. That will sound odd and not look very good but the feed-back is useful.

6. Let your jaw relax in again until your lower incisors are directly under your upper incisors (not behind). Say 'cease' again and listen. This should sound about right.

We have explored the possible jaw positions from back to front; now try from wide open to nearly closed:

7. Open your mouth wide and say 'cease' as best you can. Repeat 'cease' several times more (about three) and bring your jaw up by degrees for each one until you feel the the sound is right.

Finding the right tongue position:

8. Place the tip of your tongue behind your lower incisors and just touching the top of your gums. Say 'cease' and listen to it.

9. Raise the tip of your tongue so that it barely touches the edges of your lower incisors. Say 'cease' and listen.

10. Raise the tip of your tongue even further so that it barely touches the edge of the gums of your upper incisors. Say 'cease' and listen. This could produce a whistle.

11. Try the middle position again (as in No. 9) which should feel and sound about right.

NOTE: If you are using a tape recorder it is obviously best to record several positions at one time and then compare them on playback.

'S' can be a serious problem for those people who have new false or capped teeth. It is unlikely that they will be exactly the same size and shape as the previous teeth and the result is invariably a tell-tale sibilance that literally proclaims to an audience, 'new teeth.' The mouth needs re-educating to adjust to the new shapes and the above procedures are ideal for this. Sometimes the sibilance amounts to an embarrassing whistle, a serious complaint that is likely to cause mirth. It needs perseverence to cure it but it's worth it.

Finally, a useful comparison can be made between 'SH' and 'S'. The difference between them is that 'SH' has a slightly retroflexed tongue position and the lips are noticeably rounded. This should ensure that the distance between the upper and lower teeth is held correctly. When following 'SH' with 'S', keep the same jaw position but let your lips relax and your tongue ease slightly forward.

• Alternate 'SH' and 'S' on breath only, without voice. Keep your jaw relaxed and still:
SH-S-SH-S-SH-S-SH-S

• Compare saying the following pairs of words, minimizing any movement to your tongue and lips. Check yourself in a mirror:

SHEET	SEAT	SHOW	SO
SHIP	SIP	SHOE	SUE
SHELL	SELL	SHIRT	CERT
SHALL	SALL	SHOT	SOT
SHORT	SORT	SHUN	SUN

By now you should begin to feel what the right 'S' position is for *you*. Having found that position, you should now try to maintain it and work your way systematically through the 'S' exercises in the previous section.

The 'T & D' Factor

'T' is known linguistically as a voiceless alveolar plosive which means that, after breathing in, the front edge of the tongue rises to the alveolar ridge where it momentarily blocks the returning breath from escaping out of the mouth; when the tongue detaches itself from the alveolar ridge the build-up of air behind it is released in a mini explosion. With 'D', its counterpart, the action is similar but much gentler because it is partly voiced.

'T's' are harder work than 'D's' which is probably why they get left out in a lot of speech. Cockneys will often leave off final 'T's' - "Wha's i' go' t' do wi' you?" instead of "What's it got to do with you?" - as proof, perhaps that they are not toffee-nosed. But quite educated speakers do something similar; you will often hear: "qui..." (quite), "all ri..." (all right) and "tha..." (that). This, too, is most likely to be a subconscious attempt at not wanting to sound too precise and not wanting to alienate one's listeners. Certainly, overdoing final 'T's' invites derision so they should be touched in neatly and gently.

We have already made brief use of comparing 'T' and 'D' in the Tongue Looseners (Nos. 9, 10 & 11). Here I have added a few more for you to make the comparisons with:

> TEE-DEE-TEE-DEE-TEE-DEE
> TAY-DAY-TAY-DAY-TAY-DAY
> TAH-DAH-TAH-DAH-TAH-DAH
> TAW-DAW-TAW-DAW-TAW-DAW
> TOH-DOH-TOH-DOH-TOH-DOH
> TOO-DOO-TOO-DOO-TOO-DOO
> TUH-DUH-TUH-DUH-TUH-DUH

What is more interesting is to compare the effect of 'T's' and 'D's' on the ends of words. In the list below, the paired words are almost identical except that those ending in 'D' are noticeably longer.

• Compare the pronunciation of these pairs of words as though you are demonstrating their difference to a foreigner:

NEAT NEED   ROT ROD
WAIT WADE   FLOAT FLOWED
BET BED   ROOT RUDE
HAT HAD   HURT HEARD
HEART HARD   LOUT LOUD
BUT BUD   BRIGHT BRIDE

HOW TO CURE SIBILANT 'T'S' AND 'D'S'

I call this the 'Splashy T & D' because it does sound rather like spitting.

Again, like a shibboleth, it does let a speaker down badly. Not easy to cure, it requires a firm reappraisal of the tongue position.

Light little phrases like "Come to tea," or "What to do," sound splashy and cumbersome if the 'T's' and 'D's' are sibilant.

The problem is that the tongue is too far forward and touching the edge of the teeth. Sometimes the tongue is peeping out between the teeth, as in the 'TH' position; if you adopt this position you will see what I mean:

1. Place the tip of your tongue between your upper and lower incisors and repeat several times 'to tea' and then try 'to do' several times. The result should be dreadful.

T-19

2. Now pull your tongue in and up so that it rests against the alveolar ridge, the tip just about in line with the edge of your gums.

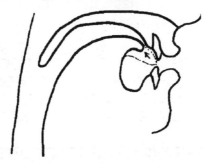

Figure 30: Tongue Position for 'T' and 'D'

Say 'to tea' and 'to do' several times and notice the difference.

3. If your tongue persists in pushing too far forward, put a clean index finger between your teeth (about half a nail's length) and say 'to tea' and 'to do' again several times, letting the tip of your tongue brush against the tip of your finger. Do this until you get used to keeping your tongue away from your teeth.

4. Go through all the 'T' and 'D' exercises in the last section, sometimes with the finger in, some time without it. Listen to yourself on tape until you feel pleased with the result.

Consonant Clusters

Consonants can be spoken singly, in pairs, in groups of three and, occasionally, in groups of four. These groups are known as clusters.

In English, most single consonants can be placed before or after any vowel, and any vowel might be preceded by one, two or three consonants and followed by as many as four consonants.

The reason I am emphasizing the subject of consonant clusters is because, in the present-day climate of laid-back speech, so much effective enunciation is lost. It is important to make people listen. All right, you may be understood if you say 'ax' instead of 'acts' or, indeed, 'fax' instead of 'facts' but you could be in trouble if you say 'sex' instead of 'sects'.

As with vowels, the number of sounds or phonemes does not necessarily correspond to the number of letters; for instance, the single letter 'X' represents the two consonants 'KS', whereas 'CH' and 'SH' are two-consonant clusters that represent one sound.

Needless to say, there are countless words containing consonant pairs, some more satisfying to say than others. Here are a few examples of words with consonant pairs that can be said with particular relish:

> plunge, bulge, twist, posting, swish, thrust, snout goblet, language, brusque etc.

Here are a few examples of triple consonant clusters at the beginning of words:

scream, stretch, splash, spruce, shrill etc.

... in the middle of words:

discreet, countless, ecstasy, illustrate, etc.

... and at the end of words:

exists, precinct, cleansed, announced, schisms, drafts, acts, sects etc.

Both 'acts' and 'sects' are quite tricky to pronounce with out a scramble. It is best to practise them by inserting a pause, first of all between the 't' and the 's': act+s, sect+s

Then try a pause between the 'c' and the 't':

ac+ts, sec+ts

Alternate these two versions a few times and the proper pronunciation should emerge clearly.

Quadruple clusters are not very numerous. Here are two examples:

instruct, twelfths

'Twelfths' is not an easy word to say, and many people will opt for the easier 'twelfs'. To get it right, try separating all the consonants first:

twel+f+th+s

... and then speed it up gradually. It should be a most gratifying word to say.

The sheer pleasure of getting your tongue round consonant clusters should not be underestimated. It is a pleasure that readily transmits itself to the listener.

Toning Up the Abdominal Muscles

THE 'IRONING BOARD'

This is an exercise I have borrowed from Yoga and it is guaranteed to wake up all the abdominal muscles from sluggishness. Two positions are possible — what is essential is that your entire back, from the tail-bone to the top of the neck, is as straight as possible and parallel to the floor. That's why I call it the Ironing Board.

> • Standing position: stand facing a firm rail or
> chair back that is approximately level with your

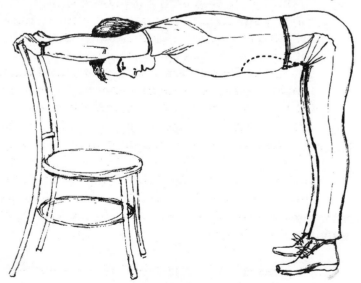

Figure 31: The 'Ironing Board' (standing)

hip-joints. Grasp the rail, or whatever it is, with both hands, directly in front of each shoulder. Now, move back, bending at the hips as you go, until your legs and back make a right angle and your arms are stretched out in line with your back. Keep your head poised so that you look straight ahead at the floor.

• Let your stomach hang loose like that of any self respecting animal. Now, slowly breathe out as much air as you possibly can and don't breathe in again until you have completed the following movements: suck your abdominal wall right in and up under your ribs, rather like weight-lifters do when they're posing (the dotted line in the diagram shows you where it should be). You may have to have a few goes at this because I find that nobody gets it in far enough the first time. You should feel as though the front of your stomach is touching your spine. When you have got the position right — minus breath hold it a moment and then, without breathing, vigorously push your abdomen out and pull it in again. Repeat this several times until you feel that you *must* breathe in - about six repetitions is the average. Relax, get your breath, and then go through the whole procedure again. Two or three goes at this is sufficient at any one time. Eventually, once a day should be enough. Remember, this is not an exercise in holding your breath *out*, but in working the abdominals in the increased space of the absent breath. Don't overdo it or make it an agony.

• Hands and knees position: the 'Ironing Board' can be done equally successfully on hands and knees though it lacks the purposeful dignity of the standing version. Also it doesn't do your best pair of pants any good. Even so, some people may prefer it.

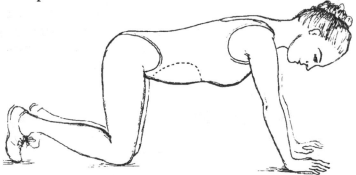

Figure 32: The 'Ironing Board' (kneeling)

• After you have done the Ironing Board several times your abdominal muscles should feel they've been used. Now you can stand upright and flex them in and out while you breathe normally. It is quite an exhilarating feeling because your guts feel so alive! Then do it walking about so that the rest of your body and limbs are independent of it.

• Finally, flex your abdominals in and out while you are talking. Say a few mundane phrases out loud as independently as you can from the flexing. Don't time the words to the muscular movements but speak as normally as possible over the gentle upheaval. The breath pulse will jerk the words here and there but just carry on. Try this also walking about.

THE 'WOOF'

Once again we follow the example of an animal's response in order to rid ourselves of the inhibitions of being over-civilised.

A dog, asleep by the fire, hearing a strange noise outside, will prick up its ears and make a sound like 'woof'. It could be a quiet 'woof' or a loud series of 'woofs'; either way, the response is visibly clear in the dog's diaphragm which will pull sharply in and up. If you watch a dog's abdomen you will see that it does not push out on a 'woof' for that would probably 'split' the sound. The dog doesn't know that but Nature does. This exercise is good for clearing the voice and ensuring the energy comes from the right source:

T-20

1. Sit in a good upright position with one or both hands on your stomach.

2. Breathe in to your waist and do a short, sharp 'WOOF' quietly and low in the voice. Don't try to be fierce, just let it come out. Check your abdominal response. Does it pull in sharply and then relax out again or does it remain stubbornly motionless? If the latter, or if your stomach pushes out, you must practise consciously pull ing it in for each 'WOOF' and releasing it immediately afterwards. After a time, this should happen naturally.

3. Now try each 'WOOF' a little louder but don't let them get rough or scrape your throat. Make sure your abdomen pulls in and releases each time.

4. Now vary the pitch — low register, middle and high. The high ones need to be loud. Note that the higher or louder you go, the more energy is needed from your diaphragm. If you try these 'WOOFS' against notes on the piano and work up towards a high 'G', you will find that the amount of abdominal energy is considerable but at no time should the throat feel involved.

Apart from its doggy connotation, 'WOOF' is a useful
'word' to use as a voice exercise because of its easy
roundness but, again, be careful where you do it. A
famous musical comedy star who is both a pupil and
friend of mine, very dignified and beautiful, was practising her 'WOOFS' in Regents Park, London, when in no
time, she found herself followed by a procession of ad-
miring dogs!

I am not alone in recognizing that animal sounds can be
helpful in releasing responses in our own voices. I
remember Noël Coward saying that when he first went
to Hollywood the voice coach there made everyone 'moo'
a lot.

ABDOMINAL MUSCLE AWARENESS

The busy young executive doing a daily workout in the
gym in order to keep the body in trim, so essential to the
image of success, can now add another dimension to the
work on those abdominal muscles that are so prided, for
they are the very foundation of vocal power and should
provide the firm base against which the diaphragm can
push. As an example of the effectiveness of this firm
base, try this simple experiment:

T-21

> • Pick up an ordinary table fork and hold it
> lightly then, with your other, free hand pinch the
> prongs in on themselves and swiftly leave go of
> them so that they vibrate. You may have to have
> a few goes to get it right but even so, the sound will
> be tinny and barely audible. Now, press the
> handle end of the fork on a firm, hard surface and
> pinch the prongs again. This time the sound will
> be surprisingly loud and not tinny. Alternatively,
> you can pinch or knock the prongs and then
> press the handle end against the hard surface in
> the same way a piano tuner uses a tuning fork.

Either way, the sound will be clear and ringing.

The same principle applies to the voice: with shallow breathing and slack, uninvolved abdominal muscles, the result will be thin and toneless, but, take a deep breath and feel the diaphragm press against those firm abdominals and the voice will be immensely improved with a good ring to it. Try it by comparing yourself, first, to the fork in mid-air:

> • Keeping the abdominal muscles and diaphragm as slack as you can, try taking a shallow half-breath. Then, as if trying to attract someone's attention, loudly call out HEY! The sound will no doubt be thin and lack carrying power. Try it again even louder without using the lower muscles. You will probably feel a nasty pull on the neck muscles and still the sound will be thin.

Now the fork pressed against the table:

> • Take a slow, deep breath until you feel the diaphragm pressing against the abdominal muscles. At the same time, with your abdominal girdle, resist the diaphragm with equal (isometric) pressure. Hold this rather pleasant tension for a moment and then, without releasing that tension, call out 'HEY'! as loudly as you can. Release the tension at once. You cannot fail to notice a considerable improvement in the quality of the sound and, after a few goes, it should be enough to halt anyone in their tracks!

This is an example of putting thought into the abdominal muscles and of putting EFFORT where it should be. The following exercises are designed to muster that power and to use it efficiently.

CONSCIOUS USE OF YOUR ABDOMINAL MUSCLES

1. Stand with your feet a shoulder-width apart.

2. Let your knees give a little and tip the *whole* of your spine very slightly forward, including your head.

This is called the 'Monkey Stance'.

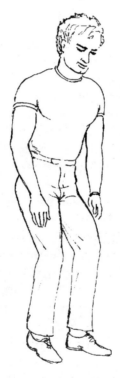

Figure 33: The 'Monkey Stance'

3. Place your hands, flat, on either side of your abdomen.

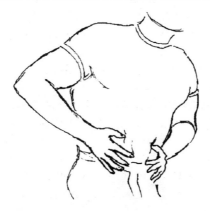

Figure 34: Hands on Abdomen

4. Let your jaw drop loosely and take in a long, deep breath through an 'OH' shaped mouth.

5. As you fill with breath, feel your diaphragm pushing against your abdominal muscles which, in turn push your hands out.

6. When you are comfortably full of air (do not raise your shoulders), hold your breath for a moment and grip your abdominal muscles IN with a pressure equal to the pressure OUT of your diaphragm (isometric pressure).

7. Without the slightest flicker in the abdominal area, release a very short, resonant 'OH' (not too loud at first). This means that, though you are releasing a modicum of breath, your diaphragm, instead of bouncing upwards as in the 'woofs', continues pressing down against the abdominal muscles.

8. As soon as the 'OH' is emitted, RELAX!

The process each time should be:
>   1. Breathe in 2. Grip 3. 'OH' 4. Relax.
>   Take care not to skimp on 2 and 4.

9. Repeat the above process, gradually increasing the loudness of the 'OH', which should always be as short as possible. There should be no feeling of strain in your throat but a pleasant, hollow sensation in your mouth.

10. Following the same preparation, do two short, vigorous 'OH's' instead of one. At the same time, check in the mirror that you don't let your lips pull in at the end of either 'OH' — this would cause a diphthong (OH+OO). There should be no visible movement.

11. Repeat the above, only this time lengthen the second 'OH' into an extended sound. This is easier and more effectively done on a definite pitch or note, loud and clear:

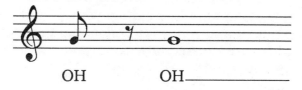

OH   OH_____

On the long note, the diaphragm will gradually want to go in and up. Even so, keep it pushing down against the abdominal muscles so that the inward movement is slow and firm. This is necessary in order to sustain the resonance right to the end of the sound. Repeat on various notes.

12. Sing the short 'OH' followed by the long 'OH'; then, without altering the shape of your mouth or breaking the sound, change the 'OH' about halfway through to 'AH':

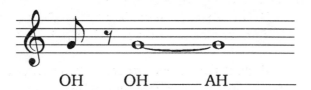

OH   OH_____ AH_____

Only your tongue should make a slight move.

13. To this last version of the exercise, add 'EE' to the 'AH', keeping the 'OH' shape of your mouth throughout. Resist the temptation to bring your jaw up for 'EE':

OH   OH____ AH____ EE_____

Repeat this at various pitches, loud and clear. (PIANO NOTES ON TAPE)

IMPORTANT NOTE: Always observe the preparation for each emission of sound with the process already stipulated:
    1.Breathe in   2. grip the muscles   3. emit the
    sound   4. RELAX.

This is hard work for the abdominal muscles and diaphragm but kind to the throat.

Tension, Relaxation and Exercise

I think it is worthwhile to pause here briefly to consider these three subjects because there is so much misunderstanding about them and, for anyone practising a physical skill, whether it be voice-work or playing golf, it is essential to get them in perspective.

TENSION

The very word 'tension' conjures up in many people's minds something that is not right and needs to be cured and they get a picture of tortured muscles and furrowed brows. We often hear of people suffering from tension but we never hear of anyone *benefiting* from tension, which is just as valid. It is true that some people *do* suffer from tension but it is equally true to say that they cannot do without it or they would end up in a heap on the floor.

There are at least three kinds of tension: physical tension, mental tension and nervous tension and, although the three are closely interrelated, it is mostly the physical tension that concerns us here.

Where physical skills are concerned, and that includes speaking, singing, walking, athletics, playing a musical instrument and a host of other activities, there are two types of physical tension; one is necessary, the other is unnecessary and can often be described as psychological tension.

Necessary tension is the flexing of muscles that actually perform the movement required for a particular activity. This may be a slight tension in a few muscles as when writing a letter, or it may be a more major tension reacting like a chain movement through almost our entire system as in a golf swing. When the writing pauses or the golf swing is completed most of the tensions should cease, leaving us with just enough strength to keep hold of the pen or the golf club and to stay sitting or standing. This tension and release is some thing we are usually very good at and don't even have to think about.

Psychological tension usually besets us when we are learning new skills or when we are using a familiar skill in an unfamiliar situation. For instance, most of us speak quite well and efficiently at home among family and friends but, when asked to make a speech in public, all sorts of unwelcome tensions are apt to arise. As for learning to sing, which is after all using the same equipment but is in effect a new skill for most of us, the most alarming tensions usually emerge. Psychological tension does not always manifest itself in the area of the main action, e.g. the throat or jaw of a singer or the wrists of a pianist, but frequently we have seen singers (and speakers) who clench their fists and twitch their fingers and we have seen pianists who continually grind their teeth. Eyebrows, shoulders, knees and various knuckles have an annoying tendency to participate in physical skills to which they have no valid contribution to make and all these tensions are wasted effort that diffuses the main flow of energy.

Tension is best measured by how little you need rather than how much and a great deal of this book is about the release of tension. This release, when referred to by instructors as relaxation, can be misleading.

RELAXATION

Relaxation is the antidote to tension and is therefore regarded by many as the good guy of the two. This is not really true because too much relaxation results in nothing happening at all. Tension and relaxation need each other for any activity, even thinking. Without the necessary interplay between them, no proper co-ordination can take place. We have often read descriptions of rippling muscles, which is what muscles should do when engaged in activity; it gives a good picture of the momentary tension in one muscle, followed by its relaxation as the tension is taken on by the next muscle and so on. Problems only occur when muscles in the chain fail to relax when they should.

Telling a tense person to relax is about as useful as telling them to drop dead. It cannot be done. Yet teachers often baffle pupils by telling them to relax whilst instructing them to do something difficult. Physical activity, whether it be doing the high-jump or having a chat, whether it be playing the piano or playing baseball, depends on this interplay of tension and relaxation between the muscles. The best example of this is the cat. A cat never wastes energy; one second he can be relaxed and the next second the claws can strike with alarming speed and accuracy.

It is true we sometimes strive to make a limb or a part of ourselves independent in order to gain greater control of it — the notorious fourth finger of the pianist or the singer's eyebrows that rise alarmingly with the top notes are examples — but this independence should only underline the fact that all parts of our system are really interdependent and that it is pointless for the musician to exercise the fingers unless the support is correct from the spine, shoulders and arms, just as it is pointless to try to release tension in the eyebrows or the jaw unless the support is correct in the spine and neck. When lying on the floor it should be even easier to release tension but there are some who find it difficult to 'let go' even then. Muscles that are constantly strained don't readily relax. Even when asleep, some people continue to harbour tension in certain muscles, as witness the grinding jaw or the clenched fists — and this is not because they are dreaming!

These unwelcome muscular tensions are so tied up with the inner psyche, that training them to be able to relax again is a painstaking process and is the basis of Alexander Technique (see P. 193).

EXERCISE

When learning a new skill or eliminating faults in an old skill (both applicable in voice-work), the burning question is how much in the way of exercise should be done, because some indeed is necessary. The answer lies in the quality of the exercising process: a carefully thought-out process, done once or twice, is worth far more than quantities of mindless repetition.

It is a sad truth that the conscientious person who practises rigorous exercises often does less well than the lazy person who doesn't worry and sails through to success. There are several anomalies in the practice of learning new skills, one of which is not to try too hard. Puffing and panting and straining do not guarantee a good result.

One of the main purposes in repeating exercises is to wake up dormant muscles and to ensure that there is a correct mental follow-through. Repetition is also necessary to impress something into your consciousness and to convince yourself that you can actually do the process required and under almost any circumstances. A certain amount of repetition is necessary for acquiring brilliance of technique in any skill. Indeed, acquiring technique requires a great deal of time and patience; I remember reading of some famous fast-bowler who, as a boy, had spent hours practising fast-spins at a strategically placed sixpence. This sort of inspired dedication pays off. The number of repetitions can be important too: never set yourself too much to do at a time or your zeal may flag before you achieve anything. It is better to practise little and often rather than too much at a time and, whatever skill you are practising, the exercises should be relevant to your daily living. Once you have got the hang of a particular exercise (or process) it is most beneficial to practice it whilst doing something else, something not too demanding like walking, tidying or pottering about.

The great composer, Franz Liszt, who was no mean slouch at playing the piano, used to do his daily exercises of scales and arpeggios whilst reading a book propped up in front of him. He said it was because he otherwise had no time to keep up with good literature but he knew it also served to prevent undue tension and the alienation that comes from over-concentration.

What I don't recommend is trying to do any serious voice-work whilst driving a car; either the driving suffers or the voice suffers — or both!

I have often been asked, "What exercises can I do to loosen my jaw?" In the same way, music students will ask their professors for exercises to loosen their wrists and there really is no answer to it. If there is unwanted tension in these places, or in the shoulders or anywhere else, exercises are not the solution. This is a pity because exercises are something positive to latch onto and it is easy to convince yourself that you have studied hard when you have spent hours at your exercises. But what is the result? Are you really any better at the end of it?

The trouble is that we tend to regard a tight jaw or wrist in the same way as we regard a rusty joint in a machine and that a little oil and waggling it about will solve the problem. But human joints are not like this and, if they are unduly tense, the reason is almost certainly psychological rather than physical. It is no good waggling the jaw or wrist a hundred times and expecting it to be loose at the end of it; the chances are that it will be stiffer than ever. If there is psychological tension and it is hampering the job in hand, then it has to be tackled in a psychological way, that is to say, by thought processes; one has to unthink the tension, to find a way of letting it go, to find the repose level, the "zero". When a muscle wants to tense up that shouldn't, we must learn to forestall it by mentally saying "No".

Of course, anyone can find a way of loosening tension in their wrists or of slackening their jaw if that is all they intend to do. The problem arises when they perform a task which may be as simple as holding a pen or speaking on the telephone. Resisting the temptation to tense up the wrong muscles and only use the right muscles when performing a task is a process that requires mental effort and patience. It is, however, the most satisfying triumph when you achieve success because you know inside yourself that *you* have done it.

A NOTE ON ALEXANDER TECHNIQUE

Frederick Mattias Alexander (1869-1955) was born in Tasmania and trained himself to be a professional reciter. Though highly successful, he developed severe vocal problems and, with no one else to consult, he searched for a method to overcome this trouble which involved a total re-assessment of his use or mis-use of his whole body. From his research into muscular usage he evolved a method of muscular re-education through thought processes which became known as the Alexander Principle or Alexander Technique. Now recognized world-wide, many colleges of the performing arts and physical training centres, as well as opera companies and theatre companies, employ a full-time Alexander Technique practitioner. Even some big business organizations and factories are now realizing how successful Alexander Technique is in dealing with the psycho-physical problems that cause so many man-hours to be lost.

Those of us who have benefited from Alexander's work can never forget the permanent debt we owe him.

Making The Most of Your Breath

Running out of breath is something mostly feared by singers. It is too shaming not to be able to get to the end of a phrase or to have to take a gulp in the middle of a word. With actors the problem is similar; they have to project the voice across considerable space and it is essential that the breath does not run out before the end of a line so that the last words are not lost. It is a common fault. How often has one heard in the theatre lines like this: "To be or not to be that is the ques...."? But even boring after-dinner speakers and ponderous chairmen should not run out of breath during their speeches even if, at times, we would dearly like them to.

In trying to avoid running out of breath it is just as much a mistake to hold it back whilst speaking or singing as it is to heave in great chestfuls of air. The point to remember is that vibrated or voiced breath lasts longer than unvibrated breath.

As we experienced in the section on humming, an aspiration of breath down the nose can only last a short time however much we might try to prolong it but if we vibrate the breath into a hum it can last a considerable length of time. The vibrancy seems to hold the breath captive.

The main causes of running out of breath are:

1. Not taking a good breath in the first place.

2. Hitting the first or second word so hard that it uses nearly all the breath you have.

3. Letting the breath out in gasps between words.

4. Insufficient vibration and resonance which harnesses the flow of the breath.

Here is a remarkably challenging exercise that should cure all four problems at once but, before we try it, let us see how good you are.

Take a good breath and slowly count out loud, from one till your breath runs out.

Make a note of how far you get - 12? 20? 30? Now for the exercise:

T-23

• Stand comfortably upright with your feet placed a shoulder-width apart. Breathe in through your mouth and nose and, instead of expanding your chest, aim at expanding your back. It is helpful to have a companion stand behind you and place the palms of their hands against your lower ribs so that you can have the sensation of pushing their hands apart with your breath.

• In the absence of a companion, you can be resourceful and do it for yourself by bringing the palms of your hands up as high as is comfortable against your back ribs.

• Breathe in and feel the breath pushing your hands apart. Now, in ringing tones, start counting slowly out loud and join the words up so that there are no gaps where breath can escape. Say the words as though they are all syllables of one vast word.

ONETWOTHREEFOURFIVE etc.

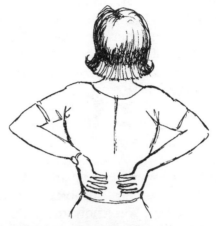

Figure 35: Hands on Back Ribs.

As you do this you will probably feel your ribs gradually collapse inwards and your breath will soon come to an end. Make a note of the number you reach and, remember, don't say them quickly in order to get a higher score!

• Breathe in again and push your hands apart, as above. Only this time, as you are counting out loud, do not let your back ribs collapse inwards but keep pushing outwards against your hands. Your stomach should gradually sink inwards with your diaphragm. Each time you do this you should be able to count a little further. Aim to be able to count to fifty but don't be tempted to hurry. The speed is a little quicker than one count per minute.

Making your breath last as long as possible is a challenge but it is not an end in itself. One needs to be able
to do it but it is not always necessary. Sometimes a
series of short breaths or phrases is more suitable to the
subject matter, or there might be a variety of long and
short phrases. If you sing a song, the rules for breathing
are more clear-cut in order to sustain the melody or
carry the sense of the words. In speaking, these rules are
not so apparent neither are they quite so vital. Nevertheless, all forms of speaking, from declaiming poetry to
social chat, are improved by an ease of breathing that
can accomodate long and short phrases.

I said that this exercise should cure all four main causes
of running out of breath that I quoted; if you know you
are going to count out loud up to 30, 40 or 50, you
instinctively know you must take a good breath. This
takes care of the first problem. Similarly, with the
second problem, if you know you are going to perform a
long, sustained phrase you are less likely to hit any one
syllable too hard. The third problem of letting air out in
gasps between words is solved by telling yourself to join
the words up. The fourth problem also needs a conscious effort in boldly resonating the voice into the facial
sinuses or the tone will not be sustained. With these
points understood, try the exercise again. When you feel
you can, try controlling the outward push of your ribs
without the use of your hands. Aim to get to 50 but don't
worry if you can't.

This next exercise works in the opposite way to the one
above:

T-24

> • Take a good breath, feeling a pleasant stretch
> in your diaphragm and abdominal muscles. Start
> to count out loud as before, only this time take a
> short breath between each numeral to replace
> the amount you have just used.

ONE✓ TWO✓ THREE✓ FOUR✓ FIVE✓ etc.

(✓ indicates taking a breath)

In this way you could go on indefinitely but up to ten is sufficient. Make sure you feel each replacement breath in your diaphragm, not in your throat.

• Now try two numerals followed by a replacement breath:

ONETWO✓ THREEFOUR✓ FIVESIX✓
SEVENEIGHT✓ NINETEN✓

The replacement breath should be commensurately larger and again must be felt in the diaphragm. Finally, and I think this is enough to get the point, take the replacement breath after three numerals

ONETWOTHREE✓ FOURFIVESIX✓
SEVENEIGHTNINE✓

The use of counting numbers may seem tedious but it has the advantage that you always know what comes next, whereas sentences have to be thought out and can hold matters up. Also, a succession of numbers requires no stress or punctuation. These two factors in particular dictate how we breathe and phrase our speech and we shall deal with that in the section on Working on a Script.

❋

Pitch and Stress

Pitch and stress are important factors in adding colour and vitality to speech. In English, they are very much inter-related though there are no strict rules for the use of either. This tends to limit the compass of English, where pitch (or intonation) is governed by personal choice or emotional demand. In a tone language like Mandarin, the compass is much greater to accomodate the very high-pitched and the very low-pitched words. In Mandarin, a word spoken in a low pitch can mean something quite different from the same word spoken in a higher pitch. Anthropologists, struggling with a primitive tone language, are apt to shock the natives by innocently coming out with a rude word simply because they have spoken it at the wrong pitch. Imagine greeting a nice native woman with "Hello, you silly old cow," instead of saying what you meant, "Hello, and how is your cow?". In English, we do not have this worry; at whatever pitch we say a word the meaning remains the same.

Pitch variation, which in linguistic terms is intonation, is the melody or tune of a voice and, whether one has a naturally high or naturally low voice, there should be plenty of flexibility within its compass to allow these variations of pitch. A monotonous voice, that is to say a voice that remains on one tone, has little or no intonation and can soon induce intense boredom or even sleep among its listeners. On the other hand, too many exaggerated changes of pitch with a lot of swooping up and down, can be extremely irritating. Either way, the listeners will tend to 'switch off' and not attend to what is being said. Similarly, stress, where we accentuate or lean on certain syllables, should be used with sensibility. It is very difficult to speak English without any stressed syllables at all though I have heard some speakers come close to it and it is guaranteed to send an audience to sleep. Conversely, over-use of stress, like exaggerations of pitch, can keep an audience awake for the wrong reasons.

Most of us alter the pitch of our voices quite naturally when speaking, especially in moments of spontaneity. If a friend tells us something almost unbelievable, and we respond with an electrified "What!", we will start the response fairly low and rise quickly in a slide:

What!

This isn't planned, it just happens. To do the reverse would b ; totally unnatural and unconvincing:

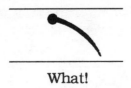

What!

As in the section on Finding Your Own Pitch you will see that I am using the interlinear tonetic transcription. The two parallel horizontal lines indicate the upper and lower extremes of the speaking pitch range and the dots correspond to syllables. Stress is indicated by the size of the dots - the stronger the stress the bigger the dot - and inflexions, or slides, are indicated by tails. It gives a very clear picture. Here is an example:

What on earth are you doing in there?

Pitch in the speaking voice can vary on one syllable in the form of a slide, which is usually known as an inflexion, or it can vary from syllable to syllable. It can also divide itself into tone groups of highs and lows according to meaning and sense.

INFLEXIONS

Inflections come under three familiar headings: T-25

• the Upward Inflection ___

• the Downward Inflection ___
and the Compound Inflection of which there are two types:
• the Rise-Fall which starts low and rises and falls,

• the Fall-Rise which starts high and falls and rises. See how these four inflexions affect the word 'yes':

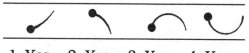

1. Yes.   2. Yes.   3. Yes.   4. Yes.

1. The Upward Inflexion characterises the 'yes' you answer when someone calls out your name.

2. The Downward Inflexion on 'yes' indicates a definite,affirmative answer.
3. The Rise-Fall Compound Inflection makes 'yes' sound even more affirmative and positive.
4. The Fall-Rise Compound Inflexion makes the 'yes' sound doubtful, as though you would rather be saying 'no'.

Both Upward and Downward Inflexions can be either short and in any part of the voice or they can be long throughout its entire compass. Compound Inflexions could be extended to more than one rise or fall but this is rare in normal speech - a bit like yodelling!

PITCH VARIATION FROM SYLLABLE TO SYLLABLE

We tend to connect rises of pitch in speech with asking questions and downward falls with answers:

Are you coming? No, I'm not!

However, this is not always the case in conversation. Alternative inflexions and the various ways we can change pitch from syllable to syllable can give a different slant to the meaning. For instance, take the following exchange: "How are you?" "Very well, thank you." The question is usually asked with a stress and a Rise-Fall on 'are', followed by 'you' dropped quite low:

How are you!

But the answer can be similarly phrased with a Rise-Fall and stress on 'well', followed by 'thank you' dropped quite low:

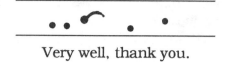

Very well, thank you.

A much deeper concern is engendered if the question is asked with the 'How' pitched high and the other two words pitched low, with the stress still on 'are':

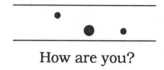

How are you?

Again the answer can be inflected in a similar way to this second 'How are you?', with the 'Very' pitched high and dropping sharply onto the stressed 'well', with 'thank you' following almost as an afterthought:

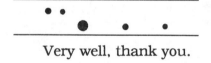

Very well, thank you.

The answer can come in many different ways, depending on how the other person is feeling and what he is pre-pared to divulge.

A very non-committal answer can be made by starting low and gently rising on each succeeding syllable with no stresses at all:

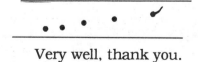

Very well, thank you.

The words are the same; the information is the same but the inference can be quite different.

TONE-GROUPS AND PITCH BOUNDARIES

Tone-groups are sometimes known as sense-groups or
breath groups and these different names give some clue
as to why there is often a sharp contrast of pitch in
people's speech. There are no hard and fast rules to fix
tone-groups and their boundaries but I would suggest
that sense is the main governing factor. Where the
subject matter is positive and cheerful the voice will tend
to stay up and where it is negative and gloomy the voice
will drop. A very clear example of this is in the opening
sentence of Charles Dickens' "A Tale of Two Cities":

- It was the best of times, it was the worst of
  times, it was the age of wisdom, it was the age of
  foolishness, it was the epoch of belief, it was the
  epoch of incredulity, etc.

If you read this passage out loud with any sense of
feeling and any feeling of sense I think you will find that
the first phrase will demand to be high while the second
phrase will automatically drop in pitch and darken in
tone. Similarly, the third and fifth phrases will be high
while the fourth and sixth phrases will be low. You could
also try reversing the pitches but I guarantee it won't
sound right.

Being aware of these tone-groups and other pitch pat-
terns should ensure that your speech always sounds
alive and interesting. I found this particularly relevant
when working with deaf people; although they had
learnt to speak every word correctly, it was not until I
mapped out the pitch levels and the tone-groups on
paper, together with the stresses and pauses, that they
sounded as natural as anyone else.

In some languages, stressed syllables are automatically
raised in pitch - the stronger the stress the higher the

pitch. In English, this would certainly be the case when shouting for help, or if one was indeed stressed, but quite often we lower the pitch on a stressed syllable as, for instance, when we tell a dog to "Get down!" 'Down' is the stressed word and is invariably pitched low:

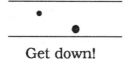

Get down!

Stress, when applied with vigour to certain words or syllables, gives them emphasis and force. In more lengthy statements, certain stresses or accents give rhythm and a lilt to what is being said.

Monotony of pitch in speaking usually goes with an almost complete absence of stress, thereby adding to the tedium. Nevertheless, there are some monotonous speakers who hit as many syllables with accents as possible, which is very wearing for an audience. Compare these three versions of the opening of a speech:

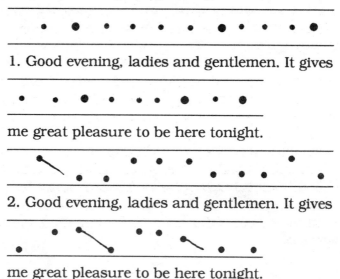

1. Good evening, ladies and gentlemen. It gives

me great pleasure to be here tonight.

2. Good evening, ladies and gentlemen. It gives

me great pleasure to be here tonight.

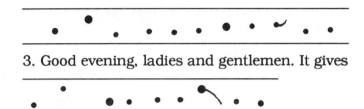

3. Good evening, ladies and gentlemen. It gives

me great pleasure to be here tonight.

The first example is monotonous in pitch and over-stressed. Even worse, I think, is the second example where lack of stress is substituted by downward inflexions. The third example should sound about right though even this could be varied in several ways.

These are just brief examples of how pitch and stress can alter a phrase or sentence. In some cases, intonation can completely reverse the meaning of a statement, as in the case of sarcasm. We have all heard somebody say the equivalent to, "Charming, I must say," when they mean the exact opposite. Sarcasm is a useful device and perfect for saying what you don't mean. However, it should only be used in fun as it can also be rather unpleasant.

In normal conversation pitch and stress usually happen quite naturally and keep the talk bubbling along yet it is surprising how many people who, when they read material out loud, sound dull and lifeless. All feeling for pitch, stress and rhythm disappear and the result is remarkably wooden. This is even more surprising when the speaker is reading his or her own script as is often the case with television reporters. The worst fault is the continuous use of downward inflexions. This sounds depressing.

For those of us who have problems with pitch, the answer is to become more aware of the possibilities of

the rise and fall in our voice and not to be afraid to use
them.

PITCH EXERCISES   T-26

1. Choose any vowel sound you like (I shall
choose OH) and slide it increasingly higher from
a low pitch:

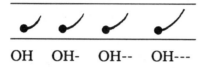

OH   OH-   OH--   OH---

2. Reverse the procedure and slide the vowel
increasingly lower from a high pitch:

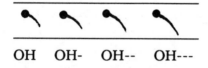

OH   OH-   OH--   OH---

3. From a low pitch, slide a vowel increasingly
higher and back to where it started:

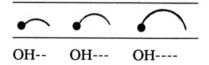

OH--   OH---   OH----

4. From a high pitch, slide a vowel increasingly
lower and back to where it started.

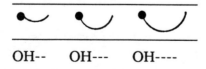

OH--   OH---   OH----

5. Choose a syllable like GO or GA; take a good
breath and repeat it seven times, rising from a low
start to a high finish like a scale of notes (don't
sing, though).

Take another breath and come down again:

GA-GA-GA-GA-GA-GA-GA˅GA-GA-GA-GA-GA-GA-GA

6. Take a phrase like "Oh, what a beautiful day", and say it with a rise and fall as though on the notes of a common chord. Again, don't sing it:

Oh, what a beau - ti - ful day.

7. Using an elongated KEE sound, take a good breath and pitch it as high as you can and slide down to the bottom of your voice. Men should try pitching it up in their falsetto register and running it smoothly down into their normal voice and so on down to the bass. Quite often, a distinct "break" occurs about half way down the slide. This happens in both male and female voices and is the natural division between the so-called head and chest registers:

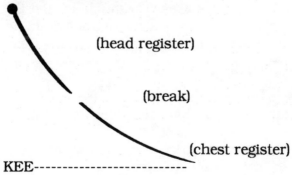

Blending these two registers so as to get a smooth transition is a necessity for singers but for speakers too it provides a worthwhile challenge. In order to do this, begin doing the exercise very quietly. Then, when it is smooth, try it increasingly louder:

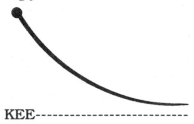

KEE--------------------------

If the break persists, don't worry about it.

8. Take a short passage from a book or newspaper and alternate each word in a high and low pitch. (I think it is better to alternate words rather than syllables or the voice may go up and down like a yo-yo in longer words.) Allow a slight pause between each word:

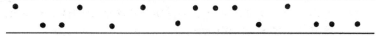

We cover a whole range of services for the profession.

This exercise goes very much against the grain because the pitches are so unnatural; nevertheless, say it through again reversing the pitches:

We cover a whole range of services for the profession.

Now repeat it once more, letting your voice follow its natural inclinations.

9. The following two passages suggest a definite pitch pattern by dint of their subject matter. The first passage should obviously start high and gradually drop to a very low pitch:

• High in the sky the birds circled round the lofty tree-tops before descending lower and lower until they disappeared into the murky depths of the leafy undergrowth.

The second passage should start low and gradually rise to a high pitch. It will also gain by increasing the stress factor throughout:

• From humble beginnings, he started at the bottom and assiduously worked his way up to become one of the most powerful men in the country.

STRESS EXERCISES

1. I think all of us have tried the most obvious stress exercise there is, if only for fun, and that is to repeat a sentence several times, stressing <u>one</u> different word, or part of one word, in succession, each time as follows:

a. To<u>DAY</u> is the happiest day of my life.
b. Today <u>IS</u> the happiest day of my life.
c. Today is <u>THE</u> happiest day of my life.
d. Today is the <u>HAP</u>piest day of my life.
e. Today is the happiest <u>DAY</u> of my life.
f. Today is the happiest day <u>OF</u> my life.
g. Today is the happiest day of <u>MY</u> life.
h. Today is the happiest day of my <u>LIFE</u>.

Each of the above versions of the identical sentence assumes a different meaning or inference through the application of the stress (or emphasis) - with the exception of (f) which has no real validity.

2. Take a sentence and alternate each syllable

with a stress and a non-stress (strong and weak):

<u>AT</u> lunch-<u>TIME</u> I <u>SHALL</u> go <u>FOR</u> a <u>WALK</u> in <u>THE</u> park.

This will sound wrong and also go against the grain as will the alternative:

At <u>LUNCH</u>-time <u>I</u> shall <u>GO</u> for <u>A</u> walk <u>IN</u> the <u>PARK</u>.

Both these versions will confirm the belief that there are probably only three stresses in the sentence:

At <u>LUNCH</u>-time I shall go for a <u>WALK</u> in the <u>PARK</u>.

3. If a sentence contains the same word twice, it is advisable not to stress either one or the other but to emphasize the words qualifying them:

WRONG: Their <u>BUS</u>iness is quite different from our <u>BUS</u>iness.

RIGHT: <u>THEIR</u> business is quite different from <u>OUR</u> business.

When in doubt about where to put your stresses (or emphases), try every conceivable way. The right way for you will soon emerge.

❋

The Solar Plexus:
Emotion and Feeling

The solar plexus is one of the principle targets of boxers due to its vulnerability. Unless the abdominal muscles are strong and ready for it, a punch there can have dire consequences on a person's sensibilities. This is because the solar plexus consists of a whole network of nerves situated in the pit of the stomach where there are also numerous blood vessels which produce great warmth. Consequently, this area has a vital effect on our feelings.

The ancient philosophers taught that the four cardinal humours (blood, phlegm, choler and melancholy) emanated from the stomach. This seems logical enough because whenever we feel gloomy or depressed we feel a heaviness in the pit of our stomachs. In the same way, when we feel excited or overjoyed, there is a lightness and an upward surge of feeling. Most, if not all, our emotions stem from this central area of our bodies which is why it is often referred to as the 'centre' in vocal teaching. Finding one's 'centre' or centering one's voice is fundamental to vocal truth and sincerity and for producing the voice that is essentially YOU.

Feelings colour the voice and make it more interesting, so it is vital that we don't cut ourselves off from them or harden ourselves against them. A speaker who is frightened of his or her own feelings is unlikely to move an audience in any way except towards the door. Reason and logic will govern the humours but an unfeeling person is not very appealing.

EMOTION AND ORATORY

The display of emotion and feeling may seem to have no
place at all in the business world. Some would vouch
that it was highly inadvisable and that business people
are not trying to go on the stage. True, but if you are
going to give some sort of speech, however modest, some
of the skills used by actors can usefully be employed.

An actor is expected to be able to project a whole range
of emotions and feelings and to have the voice to carry
them over to large audiences. A great actor can unite a
crowd of disparate individuals into a single entity by
sheer force of personality; he can twist them round his
little finger; he can reduce them to tears or to helpless
laughter.

Now I am not suggesting that a company chairman
should reduce the board of directors to floods of tears
when he or she informs them that profits for the year
have nose-dived but the gravity of the situation should
surely be heard in the voice. One does not have to rant
and rave to express feelings; the quiet and subtle utter-
ance can be even more powerful.

Great politicians and certain dictators that we can think
of have used the actor's skill in manipulating vast mul-
titudes, bending them to their will and it is interesting
to watch the politicians of today putting their points
across. With the advent of television we have ample
opportunity to assess their merits and to decide whether
we are impressed by what they say or how they say it.
They need to be very convincing in their arguments;
sincerity, whether genuine or false, oozes out of every
pore. Every trick in the book is used; the nicely turned
phrase; the exploitation of popular sentiments and,
perhaps most powerful of all, the use of their own
feelings to play upon those of the crowd. This brings us

back to the solar plexus where the gut-feeling of the speaker can produce a gut reaction in the listeners. With the breath reaching down into the abdomen, it all boils down to guts!

Whisper Technique

To whisper is to speak with completely free breath but without vibrating the vocal cords into vocal tone. As such, it is extremely useful for removing a lot of clutter from the voice. It is also very successful in minimizing the effects of laryngitis and vocal strain because it rests the voice while using the articulatory mechanism.

Whispering is very much orientated to the mouth, the nasal resonance being reduced to the minimum. Consequently, it helps to modify an over-nasalized voice.

Care should be taken when whispering that the breath is loose and that the mouth and throat are open and free. In no way should the breath be squeezed or pressurized as this will cause the throat to squeak and that would do more harm than good. The looser the breath, the more audible the whisper becomes. For freeing the voice, try the following procedure:

T-27

> • Take an ordinary phrase and whisper it in a free manner, making sure that the words are loosely aspirated below the dome of your hard palate. You could try this phrase that caught my eye in a newspaper:
>
> (whisper) Once again, there is no published manifesto.

Be quite natural with the phrase and always say it as though you mean it. Don't repeat it mindlessly.

• Whisper the phrase once or twice again then, with the same freedom of feeling, repeat it voiced:

(voiced) Once again, there is no published manifesto.

• Try whispering and then voicing random phrases of your own or pick lines from a newspaper that are fairly straightforward.

Not only is whispering invaluable for freeing the voice itself but, if you are searching for the right way to say a phrase, whether this inflection or that, whispering will often find it for you. Somehow it seems to be in touch with the inner gut-feeling which dictates how a phrase should be spoken. With this in mind, try some phrases that are more colourful, that require some show of feeling or emotion; perhaps a couple of lines from a favourite poem or even from a play. Here are some diverse examples for you to try, first whispering, once or twice, then voiced. Don't lose the immediacy of the whisper when you change to the voice. In other words, don't *think* between the two versions. Just breathe and do it.

• A couple of lines from a hackneyed epic poem:

The boy stood on the burning deck
Whence all but he had fled;

• A famous line from Shakespeare:

Friends, Romans, countrymen, lend me your ears;

• Two lines by Oliver Wendell Holmes that are strangely pertinent to my remarks about hesitancy on P. 86:

And, when you stick on conversation's burrs,
Don't strew your pathway with those dreadful urs.

• Something rousing:

Hurrah! hurrah! we bring the Jubilee!
Hurrah! hurrah! the flag that makes you free!

• Something tender by Byron:

She walks in beauty, like the night

• Or an epigram of Oscar Wilde's:

A man cannot be too careful in the choice of his enemies.

These are just a few suggestions but the possibilities are endless. The important thing is to use phrases that are short and pithy so that the repetitions come quickly after each other. Advertisement slogans are good for that very reason and, if you practise speech exercises while you are out walking (which is a good thing to do) advertisements on hoardings and passing vans provide a wealth of material.

FROM WHISPERING TO SHOUTING

Having experienced the feeling of freedom that whispering gives to anything you may care to say, we are ready now to build the voice from a whisper to a shout. In doing so, care must be taken that there is absolutely no strain in the throat. As you build the volume of sound, the only increase in physical effort should be in the area of the diaphragm and the abdominal muscles. Emotion and feeling can greatly colour and intensify the voice and, as they both emanate from the solar plexus which is very much connected with the diaphragm and abdominal muscles, no toll should be taken of the throat. This exercise is best done lying on the floor:

T-28

1. Lie on the floor with a couple of paper-backs under your head (as on P.75) and give yourself time to relax. Think of a strong, positive phrase such as 'Get out of the room!'
2. Whisper it.
3. Whisper it again.
4. <u>Mean</u> what you say, each time.
5. Whisper it again.
6. Voice it very quietly. (This can sound very menacing.
7. Voice it very quietly again.
8. Now a little louder.
9. And a little louder, directing the resonance into your facial sinuses.
10. Louder still - feel a growing anger.
11. And much louder - enjoy saying it.
12. Very loud - feel it as a release.
13. Almost shouting - muster the strength from the abdominal region.
14. Make the words longer and louder.
15. Really shouting - ringing out loud and clear.
16. Stop and relax.

If you prefer a less aggressive phrase, try something like 'I've got some wonderful news!' and build it up in the same way only this time the emotion should be one of joy, coupled with a growing excitement. Whatever you choose as your phrase, be careful where you do this exercise and who is within earshot or you might get some unexpected visitors. I was once working with a student, doing 'Get out of the room!' for all we were worth, only to discover that my dear old Cockney cleaning-lady had been wringing her hands in anguish outside the door, wondering what she could do to help.

Being able to shout in ringing tones without scraping the throat can be very useful even in business. Remember Laurence Olivier as Henry V, rallying his troops at Agincourt:

> Cry 'God for Harry! England and Saint George!'

That secured a victory against all odds.

Utilizing Faults As Exercises

It may seem contrary to recommend using faults as exercises but it can prove profitable in discovering how *not* to do things. Needless to say, these faults should not be done to excess; that would be asking for trouble. I would not advise anyone to speak in a croaky or hoarse voice for long or they would certainly regret it. A sentence or two is quite enough and teaches one a lot.

Having a go at speaking adenoidally or nasally gives one interesting feed-back; comparing a tight jaw (clamped teeth) with the over-used jaw is also highly informative.

Many younger people today speak in their throats with laid-back, husky voices, a condition that is further exacerbated by trying to shout to each other over incessant and deafening music without the vital support of the abdominal muscles. In consequence, the damage done is very difficult to cure (which is essential if they intend to do any kind of performance-speaking or singing) and, after years of grappling with this problem, I have found the best solution is to ask the student to speak *purposely* in a throaty, husky voice. This, in a strange way, immediately makes them realize what they are doing. I then suggest some words spoken in the *opposite* way, such as *clear*, and *smooth*, and *forward in the face* (any description that gives a good mental picture) and the miracle happens. *They* have found out how to make the change in a way that any amount of exercises or nagging from me cannot do. I would say it works for any fault; for instance, if you think you are inclined to gabble and are painstakingly trying to speak more slowly, have a go at gabbling even faster. That will teach you a lesson!

Experimenting with your voice and using it in ways other than its normal accepted routine can only increase its flexibility. As well as utilizing the faults for this purpose, I suggest you try putting your voice through some of the qualities listed in Different Types of Voices near the beginning of this book. Try speaking a few words in each of these qualities:

> smooth, rough, warm, cold,
> high-pitched, low-pitched,
> soft, hard, melodious, flat,
> mellow, harsh, fruity, hollow,
> husky, tremulous, raucous.

Try a few words in each of these modes of speech:

> quick, slow, precise, slovenly,
> clipped, slurred, forth-right,
> hesitant, monotonous, over-inflected,
> downward-inflected, upward-inflected.

While you are about it you could also try some of the effects of feelings and emotions:

> happiness, misery, ecstasy, grief,
> fright, hatred, love, nervousness, worry,
> anger, amusement, contempt, sympathy,
> slyness, spirituality, lust, satisfaction,
> hysteria.

Some of these qualities will be much more difficult to do than others; some will seem so similar to each other that they are virtually the same.
This does not matter. The important thing is to flex your vocal imagination.

These vocal simulations are particularly useful for actors, who need to be able to change their voices - not only for projecting certain physical or emotional states but also for complete changes of character. But this need not just apply to actors; it enhances anybody's vocal capabilities to be able to change their voices at will. And it can be quite easy: you can change your character by speaking with the tip of your tongue locked behind your lower front teeth or permanently rounding your lips through a sentence or permanently spreading them. Try it with a tape recorder; you'll have fun.

Stammering And Stuttering

The Oxford dictionary defines stammering and stuttering as almost identical conditions; certainly the effect is
similar but, to me, stammering has always meant a
temporary condition whereas stuttering is more permanent. This, however, may be just my personal view.

We have all stammered at some time in our lives due to
the fact of being nervous or tired or cold. Too much
alcohol is another cause as, although it is reputed to
loosen the tongue, more often the tongue doesn't do
what it is supposed to do after a few drinks.

For those who suffer permanently from stuttering, even
social chat can be a nightmare; embarrassment is acute
and the confidence to speak is entirely undermined.

According to recent medical reports, there is no known
cause for stuttering though some have been suggested
as possibilities such as forcing a left-handed child to
write with the right-hand, or some other childhood
shock to the nervous system. The question arises: can
it be cured? The answer in most cases is yes. On the
other hand, if there is brain impairment or nerve damage, the problem is likely to persist and one can only
hope to find some way to ameliorate the condition.
If there is no known medical explanation for stuttering,
we can at least observe what is actually causing the

stutter itself and gain much useful information on how to tackle it. For instance, it is interesting to observe how some sufferers only stutter on certain consonants: some are confined to the back of the tongue area (G, K and L), others to the front (D, T and occasionally N); some stutter on the lip consonants (B and P) and some (though fewer in my experience) stutter on open vowels. It is significant that 'S' is relatively free from the problem, due perhaps to the fact that the brain is more aware that breath has to be released smoothly to say it.

In watching and analysing those who stutter, it becomes very clear that there is some hiatus or fault in the connection between the brain and the organs of speech. The commonest form of this is when the tongue contracts almost to the point of going into spasm so that it blocks the air flow.

Every segment of speech needs a separate message from the brain to the relevant part of the speech mechanism. The messages are transmitted by way of nerves which are like miniature telephone wires except that, once broken, these wires cannot be mended. Sometimes the message doesn't get through clearly; or you get a wrong number; or the number is engaged - it is very like the telephone.

I first came in direct contact with stuttering when I was rehearsing with a young singer, a baritone. He stuttered so appallingly when speaking that I wondered how he could possibly sing the songs which were in German and not his native tongue. To my astonishment, he sailed through the songs without a trace of hesitation. And it was always so: when he spoke he stuttered and when he sang he didn't. The next time he stuttered in conversation, I asked him to sing what he had just spoken and, again, he was entirely free of it.

One can draw certain conclusions from this: that singing is usually slower than speech (though not always)
which allows more time for the brain messages to get
through; that singing is usually more efficiently breathed
(though not always) and the concept of sustaining tone
seems to prevent the trauma of tumbling over consonants. Nevertheless, it has proved to be a vital clue in
dealing with this problem.

If you suffer from stuttering and are worried by it, speech
therapists can be very helpful but, in the long run, it is
something that *you* have to do for yourself and that
means a good deal of self-analysis and re-educating
your method of speech. The following step-by-step procedures should prove very helpful:

> 1. Make a note of the speech segments that cause
> you trouble, say, 'G' and 'K' or 'B' and 'P'. Try also
> to note whether you stutter more at certain times
> than others and what the circumstances are.
> 2. Sit or stand comfortably and make sure that
> your jaw, neck and shoulders are free from
> tension. When you breathe in, open your throat
> as though you are drinking some wonderful
> elixir or take a breath of 'pleasant surprise'.
> 3. Ask yourself, "Can I breathe out freely without
> the interference of stuttering movements?" Try
> natural breathing out actions like a sigh, blowing
> out a candle, or breathing on a pane of glass to
> polish it. Satisfy yourself that you can do these
> with ease.
> 4. Take a good breath and exhale it on a long 'S'
> sound- not a hiss, but an easy 'S'. No problem?
> Good.
> 5. If you are inclined to stutter on open vowels,
> prefix them with the long 'S'. *Whisper* them first:
>> SSSSER SSSSEE SSSSAY SSSSAH
>> SSSSAW SSSSOH SSSSOO SSSSUH

Any problem? If so, make a note and go over it.
6. Now exhale the long 'S' sounds onto the same vowels,this time using your *voice*. Keep every thing very slow - the 'S' should last for at least 2 seconds. Any problem here? If so, make a note and go over it.
7. Take a good breath and exhale it on a long *whispered* 'H' - rather like a sigh, keeping your throat open and airy. No problem? Good.
8. Exhale long 'H' sounds followed by the *whispered* vowels:

> HHER HHEE HHAY HHAH HHAW
> HHOH HHOO HHUH

Any problem? If so, make a note and go over it.
9. Now exhale the long 'H' sound onto the same vowels,this time using your *voice*. Keep every thing very slow. Any problem? If so, make a note and go over it.
10. Where you stutter on certain consonants, try each one of them whispered, making the action as slow as you can - as though they are elastic and you are pulling them out. 'B' and 'G' are the most difficult to elongate but see what you can do.
11. Whisper your problem consonants - say they are 'G' and 'K' - as slowly as you can followed by the same set of vowels:

> GHER GHEE GHAY GHAH GHAW
> GHOH GHOO GHUH
> KHER KHEE KHAY KHAH KHAW KHOH
> KHOO KHUH

If there is no manifestation of the stuttering doing these, try to pin-point in your mind what you did or did not do. If the problem persists, go over it again and again and check what you are doing with your tongue and throat in a mirror. If involuntary movements occur,try to intercept them as described in the section on Tension,

Relaxation and Exercise (P. 188).

12. Repeat your problem consonants, this time followed by voiced vowels. Continue to keep them slow:

> GHER GHEE GHAY GHAH GHAW
> GHOH GHOO GHUH
> KHER KHEE KHAY KHAH KHAW
> KHOH KHOO KHUH

13. With the same eight vowels:

> ER EE AY AH AW OH OO UH

try prefixing them in turn with all the single consonants:

> B C D F G H J K L M N P Q(KW) R S T V
> W(OO) X(KS) Y(EE) Z

then the following double consonants:

> BL CL FL GL KL PL SL
> BR CR DR FR GR KR PR
> SC SH SK SL SM SN SP SY SW
> CH TH (both versions)

and a few treble consonants

> SCR SPL SPR STR

Whisper them first then voice them, and keep them slow until you feel confident enough to try them a little faster. If you are feeling really industrious, try all the single consonants *after* the vowels as well. That way you will have experienced nearly every permutation of normal English speech.

14. Make a list of words that feature segments that have caused you to stutter. Whisper them very slowly then voice them slowly. *Give yourself time to have a clear mental concept of how the words should sound before you say them.* Watch the danger points and ease them out.

15. Sing each word from your list quite loudly.

16. Choose some sentences involving problem words and sing them fairly loudly. Either sing the whole sentence on one note or make up your own tune. *Don't* take it too seriously. Have fun.

Stuttering is a condition that has to be unravelled, so go through these sixteen procedures with patience.

Metathesis and Spoonerisms

Metathesis is not a word we come across every day yet it represents something we all do quite frequently and that is to get parts of our speech the wrong way round. It has some similarity to stuttering in that there is confusion in the messages from the brain to the speech organs — particularly the tongue — and attributed to tiredness or absent-mindedness.

Metathesis consists of the transposition of letters or sounds, either within one word or between two or more words, with frequently comic results. There is not one of us who has not fallen victim to this quirk of speech. Sometimes it is the vowels that get transposed as in 'hypodeemic nerdles', or it is the consonants, as in 'freath of bresh air' (both recently heard on television). Sometimes whole words get displaced as in the rather choice 'in circum certainstances'.

Radio announcers and television newscasters are particularly prone to this aberration and in their haste have frequently made terrible gaffes by displacing vowels or consonants and the results have often been hilarious.

There are a number of well-known, "official" tongue twisters that children, in particular, have great fun in trying to get right. These often feature conflicting consonants as in "She sells sea-shells by the sea-shore". There are also some less "official" tongue-twisters that produce rude words when wrongly said and are the delight of wags who inflict them on unsuspecting victims so that everyone else shrieks with laughter. You could try: "I slit the sheet and the sheet slit me. Slitten was the sheet that was slit by me" and see how you get on. There is also a notorious tongue-twister about "pheasant pluckers".

Tongue-twisters were commonly used by elocution teachers of old as a challenge to their pupils, often without any prior training as to how to cope with the conflicting consonants. Certainly, it gave an otherwise idle pupil something to do, but mastering sentences like "The Leith Police dismisseth us" does not guarantee good speech.

Whereas tongue-twisters often don't make sense when said the wrong way round, spoonerisms, in a bizarre way, nearly always do, e.g. "He has just received a blushing crow".

The word 'spoonerism' derives from the Rev. W.A. Spooner (1844-1930), the eccentric Warden of New College, Oxford, who once announced the hymn in chapel as "Kinquering Kongs their titles take" (instead of Conquering Kings ...). One can imagine members of the congregation, tears streaming down their faces, having to stuff handkerchiefs into their mouths to prevent hysterical laughter.

The Rev. Spooner could rightly be considered the archetypal absent-minded professor and, it would seem, not a day passed or, indeed, an hour passed without a spoonerism passing his lips. Students would gleefully report the latest quotable gem, including the young man who was reprimanded and sent down for idleness: "You have deliberately tasted two worms and can leave Oxford by the town drain". Of course, many more spoonerisms were quoted than the worthy gentleman ever uttered, but the following three have the ring of authenticity: "For real enjoyment give me a well-boiled _icycle"; "We all know what it is to have a half-warmed fish within us" and "Yes, indeed; the Lord is a shoving leopard".

Getting one's tongue twisted, and spoonerisms can cause a great deal of mirth which is fine if you want to be funny but, if you are talking seriously, falling into this trap needs to be avoided at all costs. From the examples above you should know the warning signs and be on the lookout for anything that might get your tongue in a tangle, be it a quotation, the name of a product or place, or whatever. Be prepared to say the difficult words slowly or find some other way of saying the same thing. Some people have trouble with a word like 'Copacabana'; others have difficulty with 'Peggy Babcock', whoever she may be.

As any fast patter-song performer will tell you, when he's learning a song like this:

"What I want is a proper cup o' coffee, made in a proper copper coffee-pot.
I may be off my dot
But I want a cup o' coffee from a proper coffee pot.
Tin coffee pots and iron coffee pots,
They're no use to me;
If I can't have a proper cup o' coffee from a proper coffee pot
I'll have a cup o' tea!".

... you've got to practise it really slowly before you can do it up to speed.

Boundaries

WORD BOUNDARIES

The subject of word boundaries calls to mind the old vaudeville joke, 'I scream for ice cream'.

In spoken English, the running together of words into groups is common practice though there are no rules for doing so and sometimes the sense is obscured. In French, however, there are strict principles governing what is called the liaison between words; in particular, when a word starting with an open vowel is preceded by a word ending with a strong consonant, that consonant will liaise with the vowel, e.g. les enfants, il est, ton image, notre amour & etc. In Italian, if a word ends with the same vowel as the beginning of the following word, e.g. della amore, the two vowels will be amalgamated or one will be dropped (dell'amore) forging a liaison between the two words.

Both French and Italian are smooth-flowing languages which makes it difficult for foreigners to follow because of the vagueness of the word boundaries. In English, which is not a particularly smooth language, it is possible to run certain words together without obscuring the sense but this is usually because the resulting group of words couldn't be mistaken for anything else.

Such phrases as 'have another one', 'I gotta go now', 'you've a cheek' and 'he's on it as well' can all be liaised into one-sound clusters and still be quite comprehensible however quickly they are spoken. However, when speaking in public, there are certain types of word combinations that need careful consideration to avoid confusing the listener whose concentration can be seriously affected if he thought you said one thing when you meant another. The time spent correcting the error in his mind usually means not hearing the content of the following sentence.

Here are a few examples of the sort of phrases you need to look out for. You have only to compare the pronunciation of each pair, out loud, to help you decide which meaning you intend:

I scream	ice cream
a grey day	a Grade A
you and I	you and Di
ruled out	rule doubt
first aid	fur stayed
home owners	Ho! moaners
you'd hope	you dope
spirits eased	spirit siezed

It is quite clear that, by shifting the boundary (by one segment) within each of these phrases, the meaning is entirely altered. A lot can be learned by saying them out loud and comparing them.

When a word beginning with an open vowel is preceded by a word ending with a strong consonant, the best way to prevent the consonant jumping the boundary is to make a minute pause between the two words and to give a gentle glottal stop or click (ɣ) to the front of the open vowel:

and ɣI, ruled ɣout, loss ɣof, an ɣant etc.

This also helps to tone down the jumping consonant.

The same remedy applies to when a word ends with the same vowel as the beginning of the next word; to avoid their running together as in Italian, it is best to separate them with a gentle glottal stop:
see ˠeasily, they ˠache, so ˠopen, my ˠeye etc.

When a word ends with the same consonant as the beginning of the following word, discretion has to be used. If the consonants are resonant (or voiced), it is generally acceptable to amalgamate them, preferably doubling the length:
telephone number, home maker, with them, his zeal, have vanquished, whole loaf etc.

With most of the other consonants that double at the end of one word and the beginning of the next, you can either separate them with a minute pause or you can elide (that is omit) the first consonant and only pronounce the second. Try the following phrases out loud and see which you prefer:

good·deed   goo' deed
that·taxi   tha' taxi
this·sale   thi' sale
stop·pulling   sto' pulling

All of these work without having to separate the two consonants with the minute pause but for phrases like 'which cheese' or 'sick cat', the pause is necessary for clarity.

Once you have firmly planted in your mind the particularity needed for certain word boundaries, the matter should become second-nature to you and you won't have to think about it any more. Even so, consonants should not be over-elocuted; after all, no one pronounces the 'T' in Christmas. If they do, it sounds overdone.

Even with care, though, some word combinations have to rely entirely on their context to signify their meaning clearly; there is no aural difference at all in 'a tack' and 'attack' or in 'a tone' and 'atone' and one can quite sympathize with the little girl who named her cross-eyed teddy-bear 'Gladly' because she had often heard the phrase, 'Gladly, my cross I'd bear'.

> 'Cross-eyed' or 'cross I'd' - we need to know which is which!

SYLLABLE BOUNDARIES

As far as speech is concerned, syllable boundaries need not concern us so much as word boundaries. With a word like 'contentment', it is perfectly obvious where the boundaries are, e.g. con+tent+ment, but with words like 'familiarize' or 'determinable', the boundaries are not quite so clear-cut.

Syllable boundaries are more connected with spelling than with speech; knowledge of them may help decide where to put the hyphen at the end of a line of typing but it is unlikely to affect the way the words are spoken.

What is important in speech, I think, is to avoid adding syllables that aren't there, or saying two syllables when only one is intended. For instance, in one-syllable words like 'click' or 'block', it is quite easy to make them into two-syllable words by separating the 'l' from the 'c' or the 'b' so that they sound like 'c'lick' or 'b'lock'.

This is all very fine for a desired effect but, as is pointed out in the section on consonant clusters (P. 176), the consonants making up the cluster should be cemented together as closely as possible.

Examples of other words that can suffer from a fracture

between consonant clusters are: s'wim, s'narl, g'lad, c'ream, sc'ream and p'lease.

Words like 'singly' and 'ugly' are sometimes pronounced as three-syllable words without much harm being done but to put an 'r' in the middle of a word like 'drawing' is heinous. For some, even quite educated people, the 'w' is insufficient as a syllable divider and the lamentable result is 'droring'. All I can say is that it won't do!

PHONEME BOUNDARIES AND ALLOPHONES

What is a phoneme? Even the great linguistician, Daniel Jones, had difficulty in giving an exact definition because, as he himself said, the phoneme is a concept, an idea, rather than a tangible fact. Both the segment and the phoneme represent the smallest single unit of speech sound but the phoneme differs in that it represents all the possible variants of that unit. For instance, take the simple sound of an 'S'; it is quite acceptable that this is a speech unit that cannot be sub-divided but, as a unit, it can be said, for various reasons in a variety of ways, and all these variants are part of the same phoneme. A phoneme is a family of alternatives. Similarly, any vowel or consonant can be slightly changed or influenced by its immediate neighbour. Take the words 'but' and 'bud'; at first, the only difference would seem to be the 't' and the 'd' and, as far as spelling is concerned, that is so. But in sound, the vowel is distinctly altered by the presence of either the 't' or the 'd'; 'bud' is longer than 'but', other wise the two words would sound almost identical. Apart from the difference of length in the 'u' sound, the longer 'u' lays itself open to variation within its length. These variations within a phoneme are known as 'allophones', a pleasant, harmonious word invented in 1934 by the American linguistician, Benjamin Lee Whorfe.

A further example of the effect of allophones would be to

compare the three words; 'but', 'nut' and 'nun'. All would seem to have the same vowel but, on listening to them carefully, there are variants; compared to 'but', the beginning of the 'u' of 'nut' will be inevitably nasalized by the proximity of 'n', and in 'nun', the 'u' would be hard put to escape entire nasalization because of being flanked by two 'n's'. So, these three 'u's' all have allophonic differences yet belong to the same phoneme.

Even if we try to repeat the same single unit of speech-sound several times without the interference of another phoneme, as we do in many speech and singing exercises, the sameness of those sounds will only be an approximation. As we are not machines, inevitably there will be some allophonic variance.

> ☞ Try saying 'AH' nine times and see if you can make them all exactly the same. The answer is no; you can only approximate.

This is a complicated subject but one that is well worth some consideration to avoid the over-smudging of allophones across the phonemic boundaries. To reduce this smudging it is a good discipline to separate the vowels and consonants with a tiny pause, e.g.
'b•u•t' 'n• u•t' 'n•u•n' - taking as much care as possible to pronounce the 'u' vowel identically. This ties up very nicely with the Vowels-Only exercise (P. 240) which, without the consonants, removes their influence on the purity of the vowels. Singing also helps to purify or clarify the vowels because they are practised so much without the consonants and therefore acquire a stronger identity than in speech.

Consonants can equally be affected by the vowels they are next to: the 'k' sound in 'key' is not the same as the 'k' sound in 'call' because the tongue position for 'EE' is quite different from the tongue position for 'AW' and the tongue cannot help anticipating the vowel position while emitting the 'k'. Try it and see. Again it is a good discipline to practise separating the consonant from the vowel: 'k·ee' 'k·awl' and trying to give an identical, easy aspiration to the two 'k's'.

The separating of phonemes and the refining and polishing of each one before reassembling them into a string of words can result in a glittering vocal cavalcade.

Vowels-Only Technique

As I explained in the section on Phoneme Boundaries and Allophones, vowels can influence the way adjacent consonants are pronounced just as consonants can influence the purity of adjacent vowels. Here is an excellent way of polishing up the vowels:

• Choose a few sentences and read them out loud but pronouncing the vowels only. Make small pauses where the consonants would be to keep the boundaries clean. This is quite difficult at first, partly because losing the consonants is such a wrench and partly because one is soon aware that our alphabet is totally inadequate for indicating the various pronunciations of vowels. These should be pronounced as they are in the words, not as they look as letters. You may need to say some words in your mind before you can "sift" the vowels out. Take a phrase like:

It was greatly appreciated.
The vowels in this would be:
i • o • ay•ee•ŭ•ee•ee-ay•i

The 'a' at the beginning of 'appreciated' and the 'ed' at the end of it are examples of not sounding as they look, the word actually sounding more like 'uppreesheeaytid'.

Sifting the vowels is a fascinating exercise. Especially challenging are the diphthongs in words like:

expansion;   continuity;   experience;

(e · ă·ee̯-ŭ)   (ŏ·ĭ·oo̯-ĭ·ee)   (ĕ·ee·ĭ̯-ŭ)

('u' = the sound in 'cup')

More elusive are the 'unvoiced vowels' in a word like 'gentleman', of which the middle and last syllables are examples. This may bring you to ask yourself whether you pronounce 'gentleman' any differently from 'gentle-men'. Most people don't.

> • Practise the vowels-only slowly at first. Some words will be much easier than others. Where they are tricky, try limiting yourself to two or three words at a time and comparing the sound, with and without the consonants. (A tape recorder is useful here to listen to yourself.)

When you can rattle off whole chunks of vowels-only text at a reasonable speed you will really feel you have achieved something and the vowels will sound as though they have just been washed!

Highlighting Voiced Consonants

While it is hardly feasible to extract all the consonants of a text as we have done with the vowels, it is a useful exercise to read a few sentences out loud and concentrate on doubling the length of all the fully voiced consonants. These so often get scrambled over or left out altogether. Stretching them out is a good way of acknowledging their presence and ensuring that they will not be omitted so constantly, for they are valuable assets in the pursuit of clarity.

T-30

Before I give you an example, let us just remind ourselves of the main fully voiced consonants:

> l, m, n, ng, r, th (as in 'the'), v and z;
> s is frequently pronounced as a z (as in 'is',
> 'houses' and 'result') and occasionally it is
> pronounced like the French 'je' (as in 'leisure' and
> 'vision'); f is sometimes pronounced as a v (as in
> 'of'; w and y are best pronounced as 'oo' and 'ee'.

Try reading this passage out loud; the fully voiced consonants are underlined and should be held on to a moment longer than usual:

> • When I have the leisure, I like to watch television
> with a pleasant drink in my hand. Some of the
> programmes are excellent. My favourite viewing

is wild-life, music and old movies. Though I do watch the news, it is hardly a shining example of civilized progress. Even the local news is usually depressing so I switch channels like mad.

In British English not all the 'r's' are voiced but I've nevertheless underlined them all for American speakers. Note that the 'x' in 'example' is half voiced with a 'z' sound whereas the 'x' in 'excellent' isn't voiced at all.

Try identifying and highlighting the fully voiced consonants in pieces of your own choice.

One-Word Technique

This is a process of going through a text, one word at a time or, in other words, putting the spotlight on each word in turn. Whether the text is for actual use or just for practice doesn't matter, the effect is far reaching.

I started using this process long before I gave it a name. To a student muddling through a particular passage of text I would suddenly say:

> "Give me the first word."

Usually the first word would come back at me, good and clear — and better pronounced than I had ever heard it before. If not, I would ask for it again — and again if necessary, until I was satisfied that the word was well spoken. Then I would say:

> "Good. Now the next word."

The same process would continue through all the ensuing words until a suitable break would occur to stop. Sometimes two words would come out which would indicate that the discipline of separation had momentarily broken down at which point I would say:

> "I want only *one* word."

A simple enough request but, quite often, too much to expect. That is because we all become so automatic in our speaking.

Because this process involved focusing on one word at a time without the distraction of what is to follow or what has gone before, I called it the **One-word Technique** and it has had the most gratifying effect on the speech of many different types of people in all fields of work.

You could be forgiven for thinking that all this segmentation would make your speech sound stilted and wooden and that any sense of continuity would be lost but this is far from the case. In effect, each word is taken out of its setting, polished up and put back together again like a string of glittering jewels.

The **One-word Technique** has a direct parallel in musical training where slow practice has always been advocated. The idea of slow practice, however, is in many ways misleading. For instance, when a pianist practises a difficult passage slowly, he doesn't press the keys down any slower than usual, any more than a typist does when typing slowly. What he does do is to allow more time between each successive key depression. It is the same with the **One-word Technique:** the words should be spoken at their normal speed but allowing a pause between each. This pause has several invaluable functions:

> a) it prevents a mindless, onward rush of stumbling incoherence;
> b) it gives time to assess whether the word just spoken is up to standard or whether it should be done again before going on;
> c) it prevents us skimping bits of words that need to be there;
> d) it trains us to give as much attention to the

shorter, seemingly insignificant words as to the longer, more complicated words;
e) it provides a moment of recovery before going on.

Throughout all this the brain remains wonderfully alert and although it is firmly concentrating on the word in hand, it is fully aware of the word to follow. If you persevere you will find that the brain will increase its capacity for anticipating the words ahead and that you are easily able to look away from the page and back without losing your place. This makes it remarkably effective as an aid to memorizing.

I suggest you practise the **One-word Technique** recording yourself on tape as it gives you instant feed-back and is an excellent way of monitoring your progress. Play back each stage to yourself and listen critically as though you are listening to somebody else. Demand perfection.

1. Select a short text that appeals to you to practise on and read it through out loud once or twice to get the feeling and the sense of it.
2. Divide the text up into workable sections, averaging three or four lines each.
3. Focus your attention on the first word of the first section and say it clearly and completely. Pause a moment and, if you are satisfied that you gave the first word its full worth, apply the same treatment to the second word and continue word by word, with pauses to the end of the section. Watch out for any short words like 'a', 'an' and 'is' and give them their full worth.
4. Using the same section, speed up the process a little: say each word clearly and completely with a brief pause between each. There will be some mental connection between the words but, as yet,

there should be no real expression. The pitch should be lively but more or less uniform throughout. You should sound like an efficient machine.

5. Repeat the same section naturally, with your own speed and expression. It should feel very pleasing to do and a great improvement on your first reading.

6. Apply the three treatments - long-pause, short-pause and up-to-speed - to all the succeeding sections until you get to the end of the piece of text.

7. Read out the whole piece at your own speed and with your own expression. You should have the gratifying feeling that you have come to terms with each and every word and that it all runs like clockwork. If there are any weak spots, go over them again.

8. As a final challenge, see if you can say the whole piece through at double speed without slipping up.

That amount of work on a text is quite enough for one day, and you should feel satisfied at a job well done. If you continue to work on the same text on future occasions because you need it for a specific reason, go through the same procedures but I suggest you lengthen the sections rather than keep them the same.

When you have familiarized yourself with this technique, you will find that you are able to forestall yourself *before* you make an error instead of criticising yourself afterwards. This gives you a feeling of really being in charge and that in itself is most satisfying.

❋

Working On A Script

Whether you intend to use a script or not when you make a speech of any kind, it is advisable to practise on some sort of text in order to sort out the key elements that will make it come alive and have the maximum effect on an audience.

A text is useful, not only as something to practise your voice on, but also as something to practise how you would deliver such material to an audience. Thus, when the time comes that you have to give a speech that requires a script, you will know exactly what to do. With this in mind, I suggest you choose an actual piece of script to work on, your own or somebody else's or, if you prefer it, a passage from a newspaper or book. Let us suppose you have chosen something like the following piece of speech:

> • In this age of accelerating technological, commercial and social changes, we need, more than ever, to be flexible in our attitude to current trends. It is no good being oblivious to what is going on around us and banking on our past successes. We must be both alert and vigilant, and for this I want far more understanding and co-operation between the various departments. Remember, and I cannot emphasize this point too strongly, there is no success unless it is a corporate success.

Exercising Your Voice on Your Script

1. Read it straight through, out loud.
2. Read it straight through, whispered.
3. Read it straight through, out loud, again.
4. Read it straight through, out loud, with your tongue out on your bottom lip. This is to loosen your tongue by disinvolving it from the vocal activity and letting your voice travel over it to the resonators above.
5. Read it through, voicing the vowels only (see P. 240)

This is to clear the vowels, as much as possible, of the influence of the consonants. Pronounce the vowels as they sound in the words, not how they are spelt.

6. Pinch your nose and read it out loud as nasally as possible, easing all the resonance into your nose and sinuses (see P. 118).
7. Pinch your nose and read it out loud as *orally* as possible, minimizing the nasality even on the 'm's' and 'n's'.
8. Apply the One Word Technique (P. 244) to your script. As the sentences are long in our example, use one sentence at a time before going back over it for the second and third stages. The first stage is to give all your attention to the first word only and to say it clearly. Pause a moment before applying the same attention to the second word and continue word by word, with pauses, to the end of the sentence.

• In·· this··age··of··accelerating·· technological,··commercial··and··social··changes, ··we ··need,··more··than··ever, ··to··be··flexible··in ··our··attitude··to··current··trends.

Pay particular attention to short words like 'in', 'of', 'and', 'we' and 'to'; they are just as important as the long, elaborate words.

9. The second stage is similar to the first, only faster. Using the same sentence, say each word clearly with a small pause between. There should be a mental connection but no real expression, the pitch remaining more or less uniform throughout. You should sound like a very efficient machine:

• In·this·age·of·accelerating·technological, ·commercial·and·social·changes,·-etc.

10. The third stage is to say the same sentence through as quickly as possible without losing any details. If you minimize the pitch and expression it should be surprisingly fluent. Apply these three stages to the remaining sentences, or whichever way you decide to divide up your script.

Preparing Your Script for Performance

If you are going to use a script when speaking to an audience it does at least mean that you are sure to get all your carefully prepared points over. However, the effect of your speaking should be as spontaneous as possible and, in order to achieve this, four basic elements need to be considered and marked in. They are:

1. Stress, accent or emphasis
2. Pitch or intonation
3. Speed changes
4. Breathing

You may have your own way of marking up a script to indicate some of these elements but it is helpful to borrow a few signs from the phoneticians when we want to be really specific — especially about intonation. All these markings need space, so it is advisable to have your script typed with 1 ¹/2 or double spacing to allow for this.

Stress
In speech, stresses occur with varying degrees of prominence within what is called an intonation group, which may be a single word, or a phrase, or a sentence. Four degrees of stress are usually considered sufficient; they are, in diminishing degrees of strength: the Primary Stress, the Secondary Stress, the Tertiary Stress and the Unstressed. Deciding which is the Primary Stress in a sentence is usually easy and the Unstressed syllables are mostly obvious but the question of the Secondary and Tertiary stresses is often very much open to conjecture and, certainly, you can easily change your mind about them. However, in marking these stresses in a script, I think the good old-fashioned way of underlining the syllable (not the whole word) is as good as any, and you can underline it as heavily as you think the stress warrants. Only significant stresses should be marked or your script will be too cluttered. Unstresses are not usually marked.

Pitch
Here we can borrow a few of the many tone marks used in phonetics:

      ˈfor a high start
      ˌfor a low start
      ＼ sliding high to low
      ／ sliding low to high
      ∨ for a fall-rise
      ∧ for a rise-fall
      ／ for a pitch boundary e.g. high/low

Speed
Speed is usually governed by content; slow, where words are complicated or a certain gravity is required; fast,

where words are straightforward and sense will not be
lost and where a feeling of rapidity is needed. Besides
which, the contrast of various speeds keeps the interest
alive. Often the boundaries between speeds coincide
with the pitch boundaries so, if you are intending to go
faster or slower rather than normal, I suggest you mark
the boundary with 'F' or 'S'. Sometimes speed needs to
be halted with a pause which, in musical notation is
marked ⌢ .

Breathing

It is preferable not to rely on your instinct or to hope for
the best where breathing is concerned. Like any singer
or good actor, the breathing should be marked in. This
avoids running out of breath at vital moments and
ensures clarity and audibility.

The taking of breaths is mostly dictated by the punctuation and the phrasing; you might take a good breath in
preparation for an extended phrase, or breathe in just to
give one word extra emphasis. Breath intakes are best
indicated with ticks (✓).

I suggest you mark up your script in the following
stages:

> 1. Mark in all your Primary Stresses and un-
> derline them heavily. This may mean a certain
> amount of going over and weighing up, but the
> answer should soon come. Occasionally, you
> may find that two Primary Stresses occur close
> together:

Primary Stresses

In this age of accelerating technological, commercial
and social changes, we need, more than ever, to be flexible in our attitude to current trends. It is no good being

oblivious to what is going on around us and banking on our past successes. We must be both alert and vigilant, and for this I want far more understanding and cooperation between the various departments. Remember, and I cannot emphasize this point too strongly, there is no success unless it is a corporate success.

> 2. Mark in your Secondary Stresses, and then, if there are any, your Tertiary Stresses. Depending on how you feel about a phrase at a given moment, you may find yourself shifting these two around before making a decision:

Add Secondary and Tertiary Stresses

In this age of accelerating technological, commercial and social changes, we need, more than ever, to be flexible in our attitude to current trends. It is no good being oblivious to what is going on around us and banking on our past successes. We must be both alert and vigilant, and for this I want far more understanding and co-operation between the various departments. Remember, and I cannot emphasize this point too strongly, there is no success unless it is a corporate success.

> 3. Before considering the Intonation and the Speed Changes, I think it is best to mark the breaths in next. I have been rather sparing here and you may feel you need to take more, in which case, you can take extra breaths where there are commas (except the one after the word 'technological' which would break the flow), or before an 'and'. An extra breath could also be taken between the two words 'co-operation' and 'between', depending on how you phrase it. The important thing is to mark the

main breaths; you can always pop in a few
more, later:

Breathing

In this age of accelerating technological, commercial
and social changes, we need, more than ever, to be
flexible in our attitude to current trends. It is no good
being oblivious to what is going on around us and
banking on our past successes. We must be both alert
and vigilant, and for this I want far more understanding
and co-operation between the various departments.
Remember, and I cannot emphasize this point too
strongly, there is no success unless it is a corporate
success.

4. Put in your Intonation marks. This particular piece of script lies mostly in the middle of
the intonation scale, with a few highs and
lows. I think the first sentence should start
fairly high and gradually descend in pitch to
the word 'trends'. Within that sentence there is
one parenthesis, 'more the ever', which requires a slight drop in pitch. the word 'alert'
should slide upwards and contrast with 'vigilant' sliding down. There is a very distinct and
long parenthesis after 'Remember' which
should drop quite low as far as 'strongly'; 'there
is' should pick up the pitch of 'Remember' to
make it quite clear to the listener. The piece
ends with a downward but positive emphasis:

Intonation

In this age of accelerating technological, commercial
and social changes, we need, more than ever, to be
flexible in our attitude to current trends. It is no good

being oblivious to what is going on around us and banking on our past successes. We must be both alert and vigilant, and for this I want far more understanding and co-operation between the various departments. Remember,/ and I cannot emphasize this point too strongly,/there is no success unless it is a corporate success.

> 5. Mark in your Speed Changes. Not a great deal of variation here, except to tread carefully through the longer words. A pause after 'Remmember' and another one after 'strongly' will emphasize the parenthesis and make it more dramatic:

Speed Changes

In this age of accelerating technological, commercial and social changes,we need, more than ever, to be flexible in our attitude to current trends.It is no good being oblivious to what is going on around us and banking on our past successes. We must be both alert and vigilant, and for this I want far more understanding and co-operation between the various departments. Remember, and I cannot emphasize this point too strongly, there is no success unless it is a corporate success.

Your script should finally look something like this:

In this age of accelerating technological, commercial and social changes,we need,/ more than ever,/ to be flexible in our attitude to current trends. It is no good being oblivious to what is going on around us and banking on our past successes./We must be both alert and vigilant, and for this, I want far more understanding and co-operation between the various departments. Remember, and I cannot emphasize this point too strongly, there is no success unless it is a corporate success.

When you actually come to perform your script as opposed to rehearsing it or running it through, you should have no need to refer to all the signs and hieroglyphics any more. The work will have been done. All that should catch your eye are the main breath marks and the main stresses.

Memorizing a Script
You will probably not need to memorize a complete script, verbatim. However, to know it almost off by heart gives great assurance.

The human memory is a miraculous phenomenon but it doesn't like being pressurized. It is no good ramming things into it or gabbling texts through, over and over again, in order to learn them. The brain needs to be in a free and easy state in order to receive and store the information. How often have we desperately tried to learn something and nothing has gone in and at other times, not tried at all and the thing has stuck. F. Mattias Alexander (see P. 193) maintained that concentration that calls for effort alienates the brain from the subject. I think we all know the feeling.

In order to memorize anything, be it facts and figures or a speech or a poem, it is best to *let* the information in at a leisurely pace and not consciously try to learn it at all but leave it to the subconscious. Difficult for those who are conscientious and want to *work*. This is where the One-Word Technique comes in again because you *are* working but at a leisurely pace and the result is quicker.

By pausing between each word, the brain has time to absorb it while considering the next word.

The One-Word Technique for memorizing is a little more extended than it is for word clarity, a couple of pages back, the main difference being that, after the first stage, you will consciously look ahead as specified. Always divide a long script into suitable lengths before applying the treatment to the entire piece. Do each length in three stages:

1. Give all your attention to the first word and say it clearly. Pause a moment before applying the same attention to the second word and continue word by word with pauses to the end of the section.

2. Say the first word clearly with your eye on the second word. Continue saying each word separately with a small pause between each and keeping your eye *one word ahead.* There should be a mental connection but no real expression, the pitch remaining more or less uniform throughout.

3. Say the first word clearly with your eye on the next three or four words. Continue saying each word separately with a small pause between each and keeping your eye several words ahead.

4. Now apply all three stages to the whole script or, if you prefer it, just apply stage three. By now your brain will be impatient. You will be surprised how often you can lift your eyes from the page, having always absorbed several words in advance. A mere glance down will keep the ball rolling.

5. Do the whole script through double speed — several times if necessary. Make yourself keep going.

6. Do the whole script through as you would like to deliver it to an audience, sometimes leisurely and sometimes speedily, with plenty of colour and nuance. Glance at the script only when necessary.

You can apply any of these stages to your script as many times as you like but, even if you have only time to apply the first stage, you will find it makes a tremendous improvement in your grasp of the material.

A Short Daily Workout

A short daily workout is a good habit to acquire; short, because you are more likely to do it. If you set yourself a long workout it is so easy to tell yourself that you haven't got time to do it. Any form of good preparatory vocal exercise is better than none. So, a short workout to which you can add any other exercises you like when you have the time.

It would be ideal to start every workout with lying on the floor but this is not always convenient and it does require more time. However, as I said earlier, when things are stressful, the best thing you can do is to lie flat on the floor and do nothing. Leaving the lying down procedures (P. 75) to days when you are suitably dressed and not in a hurry, the following daily workout is drawn from many exercises that have been described elsewhere in this book in greater detail and at greater length:

T-32

1. Stand in an easy upright position with your feet about a shoulder-width apart and your weight evenly distributed between them. (P. 66)
2. Take an easy deep breath and raise both arms loosely until they are above your head. Feel your chest rise naturally, lifting your ribs

away from your waist and making as much space as possible between your ribs and your hips. Now stretch your arms until they are straight, right to the fingertips. Breathe in right down to your waist.

3. As you breathe out, relax your fingers, then your hands, followed by your wrists and elbows until your upper arms are level with your shoulders.

4. Keeping your elbows at shoulder level, ease them back as far as they will comfortably go. Feel your chest open out and consciously breathe into it.

5. Still keeping your elbows level with your shoulders, bring them slowly forwards until they almost meet in front of you. As you do so, let the top of your spine curl forward and your head drop down a little. Feel your back open out and consciously breathe into it.

6. Uncurl your spine to its upright position, bringing your head with it. Let your arms fall loosely to your sides, leaving your chest buoyant.

7. Release the tension in your neck muscles so that your head falls forward, your chin almost on your chest. (P. 69)

8. Slowly revolve your head twice each way, letting your jaw fall open as your head goes back. Finish in the starting position (looking at the floor).

9. With the back muscles of your neck, slowly bring your head up to level so that you are looking straight ahead of you. Pause. Leaving your jaw loose, gradually relax those neck muscles so that your head slowly falls back. Feel the separation from your jaw.

10. Lengthening the back of your neck, bring your head slowly up to level again. Feel it

coming towards your jaw - don't let your jaw come to it. Pause.

11. Relax your head slowly forward again and repeat the rocking backwards and forwards several times, bearing in mind that when your head is dropped forward your mouth is virtually closed, and when it is dropped back your mouth is open in a natural gape.

12. Drop your head forwards and let the weight of it pull your spine down like a drooping plant. (P. 70) As you curl down your spine, let your shoulders relax and your arms hang loose. Keep your balance by letting your knees bend a little.

13. As you hang down from your waist, gently shake your head, shoulders and arms. Pause long enough to feel how heavy your head is then slowly uncurl your spine, letting your shoulders and arms fall into place, your neck and head coming up last.

14. Let your head fall back leaving your mouth open. Raise the back of your tongue against your soft palate and do about seven whispered 'GA's' on a long breath *in* (P. 72), and the same number of whispered 'K's' on the breath *out*. Repeat several times.

15. Make an easy vocal sound (UH) and flop down your spine till you are hanging from your waist (P. 83). Keep renewing the sound as you flop about, hanging from your waist. Renew the sound again and unroll your spine, flopping your head and shoulders gently until you are upright.

16. Take a deep, easy breath and release it on a long sustained sound in the middle of your voice and with loosely clenched fists, gently pummel the top of your chest and down your breast-bone (P.84).

17. Take a deep, easy breath and release it on a leisurely, whispered 'HA' (P. 80). Repeat several times.

18. Let your head fall back, take a breath and say low in your voice: HA-HA-HA. Follow on with the 'HA-HA-HA-HER-HER-HER-HEE-HEE-HEE' exercise (P. 99) with the three pitches: low, medium and high; and the three head positions: back, level and forward. Then reverse it: 'HEE-HEE-HEE-HER-HER-HER-HA-HA-HA' with the three pitches: high, medium and low; and the three head positions: forward, level and back. Repeat several times.

19. Follow on with the 'HA-ER-EE' glissando, sliding *up* with your head moving forwards; then reverse it, 'HEE-ER-AH', sliding *down* with your head moving back (P. 101).

20. Let your knees go slack and your head and shoulders loose. Using your natural breathing rhythm, breathe out on whispered 'HER's' (P. 89). When you feel like it, change to quietly voiced 'HER's' (one per breath); gradually make each 'HER' a little louder until you feel the need to change to a bright 'HAY'. Feel bright-eyed and cheerful, your face smiling. Move about as you increase the volume and the length of the 'HAY's' until they are as loud as you feel you can go (depending on who your neighbours are). If you can, continue calling out the 'HAY's' to that imaginary friend in the distance until they sound like prolonged cheers, but remember, *no straining*.

After this, you should feel really good and fit for anything. On those days when you've got time to do more, choose which direction to take - Resonance or Diction or Abdominal work. Choose a favourite exercise or work on your weak spots. Do something different each day.

Can't Find The Time?

There is always a problem for busy people who want to improve certain skills but who, when it comes to it, can't find the time; there are the career demands, the family demands and the social demands, so that the whole project gets squeezed out or left perennially 'till tomorrow'. Then there is the problem of finding somewhere private to practise these skills— a little golf on the office carpet is allright but vocal exercises can sound very peculiar to the uninitiated. Even at home, it is not always a simple matter to shut oneself away and be completely uninhibited; if there are children around, great curiosity will be aroused if 'HO' and 'HUM' can be heard coming from Mummy or Daddy's room. If children are the problem, I have always recommended trying out some of the exercises on them; they love doing 'pinched EE's' and blowing 'blubber lips' and you can all have a good laugh.

Even for those who are eager to get on, not finding the time is the classic excuse for not doing any 'homework'. Yet, however busy we are, it is surprising how much time we spend not being fully occupied; even within our work schedule we spend a great deal of time waiting - waiting for someone to answer the phone; waiting for transport to arrive; waiting to see someone; waiting for the lift; waiting at the traffic lights and so forth. All these idle moments provide ideal opportunities for trying out some of the exercises to improve your voice. Of course, suitable exercises need to be chosen for the location; one wouldn't erupt into loud 'HA's' in a crowded lift (elevator), but snatching moments (as I call them) has the double advantage of making use of wasted time and of incorporating the exercises into your everyday life. If anything, this is more valuable than a great deal of formal practice sessions.

Singing in the bath or shower has long been a proverbial pastime; men, particularly tend to lose all inhibitions while soaking or soaping in the resonant confines of the bathroom, the steam unleashing many would-be Pavarottis. Strangely enough, I've yet to hear a good soprano in the bath, but perhaps I've led a sheltered life. In any case, doing some serious voice work in the bath or shower is much to be recommended and while you're about it you might take a look at those abdominal muscles in the mirror!

With location and opportunity in mind, I have categorized some of the exercises under headings indicating volume (from silent to very loud), and visibility (discernible to persons nearby or not).

CATEGORIZATION OF EXERCISES
    Silent and Invisible - ideal for waiting in
    public places:
    Posture: spine lengthening; sitting and standing.
    Some breathing exercises.
    Jaw looseners behind closed lips.
    Soft palate awareness.
    Tongue looseners.
    Using the diaphragm and abdominal muscles.
    Silent but Visible - ideal for doing in rooms
    next to inquisitive or complaining neighbours:
    All posture exercises.

All breathing exercises.
Whispered 'HA's'
Shaking out - without sound.
Tongue looseners and lip looseners.
The 'Ironing Board'.
Whispering - not quite silent but near enough.
Quiet and Fairly Invisible - ideal when out
walking:
Exploring the bottom of the voice.
Humming.
Vibrato - dots and pulses.
Whispered 'HA's'
Loud and Fairly Invisible - ideal while walk-
ing in noisy surroundings and when jogging:
'HAY's' and 'HA's'.
Abdominal 'HAY's' (pulling in).
Shaking sound out (while jogging).
Loud and Visible - best done in private so that
you can be uninhibited:
Drumming and Pummelling.
HA-HA-HA HER-HER-HER HEE-HEE-HEE
Conscious Use of the Hard Palate.
Build-up of sound - from quiet 'HER's' to loud
'HAY's'.
The 'Woof'.

I could specify many more examples but would rather
leave it to your ingenuity to do what you can.

✳

Self Assessment

At the end of this book I would like you to ask yourself,
"Have I learnt anything and, if so, can I put it into
practice?" Having put it into practice, do not underesti-
mate yourself; even if you have only improved the saying
of one word, you have achieved something; even if you
have only improved your ability to listen to other people,
you have achieved much. But having spoken in any
significant capacity, you should then ask yourself: "I
have had my say. Have my listeners heard me and, if so,
did they understand what I said?" Let us hope the
answer is yes! One cannot wish for more.

GLOSSARY

Allophone — a variant of a vocal sound or phoneme, usually caused by its immediate proximity to a conficting sound, thereby causing a slight distortion.

Alveolar ridge — the ridge-like border of the upper (and lower) jaws containing the sockets of the teeth. For vocal purposes, only the upper alveolar ridge is referred to.

Diphthong — a single speech sound consisting of two vowel sounds joined by a glide.

Elision — to elide. The emission of a vowel, consonant or syllable in pronunciation, e.g. t'other.

Epiglottis — the leaf-like lid which covers the glottis (q.v.) during swallowing, preventing the entrance of food or drink into the larynx.

Falsetto — higher than normal pitching of the voice achieved by vibrating only half the length of the vocal cords. Most noticeable in the male voice but equally possible with women.

Fundamental — the root of a sound which generates a series of harmonics.

Glottal stop — releasing a word or sound with a sudden opening of the vocal cords causing a slight shock or 'bump', rather like a small cough.

Glottis — the opening between the vocal cords. The glottis is a space, not an object.

Harmonics — a series of oscillations or vibrations in which each oscillation has a frequency that is an integral multiple of the fundamental frequency (q.v.).

Hyoid bone — the U-shaped bone at the root of the tongue.

Incisors — the four front teeth, both upper and lower, used for cutting and gnawing.

Isometric pressure — pitting equal strength of one force against another, particularly muscular strength.

Liaison — a binding or joining of units. Vocally, this is joining the end of one word with the beginning of the next.

Linguistics — the science of language.

Monophthong — a vowel retaining the same sound throughout its duration.

Mylohyoid muscle — a flat triangular muscle connected with the hyoid bone and the front of the jaw bone that forms the floor of the mouth.

Obicularis oris — the circular muscle surrounding the mouth behind the lips.

Oesophagus or esophagus — the muscular passage connecting the mouth and pharynx with the stomach.

Phoneme — the smallest unit of speech but representing every possible variant of that unit.

Phonetics — pertaining to speech sounds, their production and transcription in written symbols.

Plosive — similar in effect to explosive; a speech sound released with sudden force, like a 'pop'.

Retroflexion — the tip of the tongue curled upwards and back.

Segment — the smallest indivisible unit of speech. It differs from the phoneme in that it does not represent a family of variants.

Shibboleth — a peculiarity of pronunciation that distinguishes or marks a particular group of people. It can also be a test word or phrase to identify or stigmatize certain people. Shibboleth is a Hebrew word and in the Old Testament refers to the word 'freshet' which the Ephraimites could not pronounce properly. As a result they were identified by their enemies the Gileadites and slain — all because they could not pronounce the sound 'sh' (see Judges 12:4-6).

Sub-lingual frenum — the membrane under the tongue that restricts its motion like a bridle.

Trachea — the windpipe, the tube extending from the larynx to the bronchi for conveying air to and from the lungs.

Triphthong — a single speech sound consisting of three vowels connected by glides.

Upper partials — overtones or harmonics (q.v.) which are higher in frequency than the fundamental (q.v.).

Velum — another word for the the soft palate.

Bibliography :

— BARLOW, Wilfred, The Alexander Principle (1975), Arrow Books Ltd, U.K.

— CRUTTENDEN, Alan, Intonation (1985), Cambridge University Press, Cambridge, U.K.

— HARVEY, Christine, Secrets of the World's Top Sales Performers (1990), Bob Adams Inc., Holbrook, MA

— JONES, Daniel, The Phoneme; It's Nature and Use (1967) 3rd Edition, Cambridge University Press, Cambridge U.K.

— KENWORTHY, Joanne, Language in Action, An Introduction to Modern Linguistics (1991), Longman Group Ltd.

— O'CONNOR, J.D., Phonetics (1978) Penguin Books, Harmondsworth, U.K.

— O'CONNOR, J.D. and ARNOLD, G.F., Intonation of Colloquial English (1973) 2nd Edition, Longman Group

About the Author:

John Dalby was born in Bristol, England and is the son of a doctor and grandson of a celebrated Methodist preacher. At age 18, he started in the theatre at the Bristol Old Vic where he acted, painted scenery and wrote music. Later he went to London to take a musical degree, followed by vocal study in Munich, Germany.

He has always worked as a performer, making his first appearance on television playing Gershwin's "Rhapsody in Blue" and took over from Dudley Moore in "Beyond the Fringe". He has written and appeared in several successful musicals and revues. In films, he worked on "Death on the Nile", "Evil Under the Sun" and "The Mirror Crack'd" in which he had brief scenes with Elizabeth Taylor and Angela Lansbury. In "Stories From a Flying Trunk" he arranged Rossini's music for a ballet choreographed by Sir Frederick Ashton which is now in the Royal Ballet repertoire. He worked for five months in India with Sir David Lean on the film "A Passage to India". His one-man show, "Colley Cibber - The Man Who Re-wrote Shakespeare" has been performed in many parts of the world.

From his experience as a performer, he gleaned much insight into the workings of the voice, and became fascinated with solving other people's problems. He became the first musical director of the London Academy of Music and Dramatic Art where he worked as assistant to the great voice teacher, Iris Warren, who was responsible for setting him on course to impart his knowledge of vocal skills. Since then, John Dalby has taught, lectured and given demonstrations throughout the United Kingdom and various parts of the world. For a time he taught voice at the Actors' Centre, London, before going to Australia to teach voice and singing at the Western Australian Academy of Performing Arts. At home, he has a large clientele of students ranging from actors and singers to television reporters and numerous middle management and executive business representatives.